PUPPIES OR POPPIES?
ESL BINGO

Elizabeth Kuizenga Romijn

illustrated by Tamara Romijn

Command Performance Language Institute
1755 Hopkins Street
Berkeley, CA 94707-2714
USA
Tel/Fax: 510-524-1191
Email consee@aol.com
http://hometown.aol.com/commandperform1/myhomepage/business.html

PUPPIES OR POPPIES?
ESL BINGO
is published by the
Command Performance Language Institute,
which features
Total Physical Response products
and other fine products
related to language acquisition and teaching.

DISTRIBUTORS

of Command Performance Language Institute materials

Clarity Language Consultants Ltd
(Hong Kong and UK)
PO Box 163, Sai Kung,
HONG KONG
Tel (+852) 2791 1787, Fax
(+852) 2791 6484
www.clarity.com.hk

Tempo Bookstore
4905 Wisconsin Ave., N.W.
Washington, DC 20016
(202) 363-6683
Fax (202) 363-6686
Tempobookstore@usa.net

Multi-Cultural Books & Videos
28880 Southfield Rd.,
Suite 183
Lathrup Village, MI 48076
(248) 559-2676
(800) 567-2220
Fax (248) 559-2465
service@multiculbv.com
www.multiculbv.com

Secondary Teachers' Store
3519 E. Ten Mile Rd.
Warren, MI 48091
(800) 783-5174
(586)756-1837
Fax (586)756-2016
www.marygibsonssecondaryteachersstore.com

Carlex
P.O. Box 81786
Rochester, MI 48308-1786
(800) 526-3768
Fax (248) 852-7142
www.carlexonline.com

Miller Educational Materials
P.O. Box 2428
Buena Park, CA 90621
(800) MEM 4 ESL
Free Fax (888) 462-0042
MillerEdu@aol.com
www.millereducational.com

Continental Book Co.
80-00 Cooper Ave. #29
Glendale, NY 11385
(718) 326-0560
Fax (718) 326-4276
www.continentalbook.com

Authors & Editors
10736 Jefferson Blvd. #104
Culver City, CA 90230
(310) 836-2014
authedit@mediaone.net

David English House
6F Seojung Bldg.
1308-14 Seocho 4 Dong
Seocho-dong
Seoul 137-074
KOREA
Tel 02)594-7625
Fax 02)591-7626
hkhwang1@chollian.net
www.eltkorea.com

Midwest European Publications
915 Foster St.
Evanston, IL 60201-3199
(847) 866-6289
(800) 380-8919
Fax (847) 866-6290
info@mep-eli.com
www.mep-eli.com

Teacher's Discovery
2741 Paldan Dr.
Auburn Hills, MI 48326
(800) TEACHER
(248) 340-7210
Fax (248) 340-7212
www.teachersdiscovery.com

Edumate
2231 Morena Blvd.
San Diego, CA 92110
(619) 275-7117
Fax (619) 275-7120
edumate@aol.com

BookLink
465 Broad Ave.
Leonia, NJ 07605
(201) 947-3471
Fax (201) 947-6321
booklink@intac.com
www.intac.com/~booklink

Sosnowski Language Resources
58 Sears Rd.
Wayland, MA 01778
(508) 358-7891
(800) 437-7161
Fax (508) 358-6687
orders@SosnowskiBooks.com
www.sosnowskibooks.com

World of Reading, Ltd.
P.O. Box 13092
Atlanta, GA 30324-0092
(404) 233-4042
(800) 729-3703
Fax (404) 237-5511
polyglot@wor.com
www.wor.com

Berty Segal, Inc.
1749 E. Eucalyptus St.
Brea, CA 92821
(714) 529-5359
Fax (714) 529-3882
BertySegal@aol.com
www.tprsource.com

Entry Publishing & Consulting
P.O. Box 20277
New York, NY 10025
(212) 662-9703
Toll Free (888) 601-9860
Fax: (212) 662-0549
lyngla@earthlink.net

International Book Centre
2391 Auburn Rd.
Shelby Township, MI 48317
(810) 879-8436
Fax (810) 254-7230
ibcbooks@ibcbooks.com
www.ibcbooks.com

Canadian Resources for ESL
15 Ravina Crescent
Toronto, Ontario
CANADA M4J 3L9
(416) 466-7875
Fax (416) 466-4383
Thane@interlog.com
www.interlog.com/~thane

Sky Oaks Productions
P.O. Box 1102
Los Gatos, CA 95031
(408) 395-7600
Fax (408) 395-8440
TPRWorld@aol.com
www.tpr-world.com

Alta Book Center
14 Adrian Court
Burlingame, CA 94010
(650) 692-1285
(800) ALTAESL
Fax (650) 692-4654
Fax (800) ALTAFAX
info@altaesl.com
www.altaesl.com

SpeakWare
2836 Stephen Dr.
Richmond, CA 94803
(510) 222-2455
leds@speakware.com
www.speakware.com

Calliope Books
Route 3, Box 3395
Saylorsburg, PA 18353
Tel/Fax (610) 381-2587

European Book Co.
925 Larkin St.
San Francisco, CA 94109
(415) 474-0626
Toll Free (877) 746-3666
info@europeanbook.com
www.europeanbook.com

Applause Learning Resources
85 Fernwood Lane
Roslyn, NY 11576-1431
(516) 365-1259
(800) APPLAUSE
Toll Free Fax
(877) 365-7484
applauselearning@aol.com
www.applauselearning.com

Delta Systems, Inc.
1400 Miller Parkway
McHenry, IL 60050
(815) 36-DELTA
(800) 323-8270
Fax (800) 909-9901
custsvc@delta-systems.com
www.delta-systems.com

Multi-Cultural Books & Videos
12033 St. Thomas Cres.
Tecumseh, ONT
CANADA N 8N 3V6
(519) 735-3313
Fax (519) 735-5043
service@multiculbv.com
www.multiculbv.com

Independent Publishers International
Kyoei Bldg. 3F
7-1-11 Nishi-Shinjuku,
Shinjuku-ku, Tokyo
JAPAN
Tel +81-0120-802070
Fax +81-0120-802071
contact@indepub.com
www.indepub.com

Continental Book Co.
625 E. 70th Ave., Unit 5
Denver, CO 80229
(303) 289-1761
Fax (800) 279-1764
cbc@continentalbook.com
www.continentalbook.com

First edition published November, 1998
Second printing September, 2002

Printed in the USA on 50% recycled, acid-free paper with soy-based ink.

ISBN 0-929724-42-9

contents

preface

Bingo? Until I began teaching ESL in San Francisco several decades ago, Bingo was just a boring game involving five measly letters, hundreds of redundant numbers, and just dumb luck. After fellow ESL teacher Silvia Ericson introduced to me the concept of Bingo for the purposes of reviewing ESL vocabulary, my imagination and my linear mind began to get together after classes on Thursdays to contrive some amusements to keep the students engaged on Fridays while at the same time focused on reinforcing what we had gained during the week.

The resulting Bingo games finally grew into such a large and diverse collection that after a while I knew I needed to share them with other teachers. Not until now have I actually taken the time to gather them together and put them all down on paper. I may not be finished yet, as I continue to come up with ideas of how to fit material into this format that many students find so appealing.

Please email me at **elizabethk@pacbell.net** to let me know how these games and lessons work for you and your students. Any suggestions or comments you have about the instructions, lessons, or the games themselves will be gladly received. I especially welcome input with regards to which Phonology Bingo games in Section Three are challenging to the language groups with which you are familiar.

Bingo isn't for every class. Some students respond better to Friday quizzes and exams. But most students thoroughly enjoy Bingo, looking forward to these games all week long. They also improve their listening comprehesion and their spelling, and reinforce newly acquired grammatical features and vocabulary thru playing the games and doing the activities that lead into them. Give Bingo a try, and *have fun!*

EKR
Oakland, California
Summer, 1998

acknowledgments

Thank you, **Silvia Ericson**, for the concept of ESL Bingo so many years ago.

Many, many thanks to **Contee Seely** for *always* being available to comment, teach computer techniques, provide resources, proofread, encourage, and most importantly, to *publish this book!*

I'm particularly thrilled that my daughter **Tamara Romijn** returned from her post-graduate world travels in time to illustrate Puppies or Poppies. Thank you, Tamara, not only for enlivening these pages with your drawings, but also for contributing many other valuable suggestions for changes in wording and format.

For valuable input about the Chinese Languages named in Section Three, special thanks to **Frank Yee** and **Dr. Bingkun Hu**.

For skillful, thoughtful comments about the entire book, many thanks to **Denise Jindrich**. Your expertise as a resource instructor is greatly valued.

For help with the wording on some of the games in Section Three, special thanks to my nephew **Marcus Liefert**.

I'm grateful to the **San Francisco Community College District** for granting me the sabbatical time to write this book.

And thanks to all **my students** for their enthusiastic reception of these games and for always making it clear what does and does not work.

Thank you, **Larry Statan** for taking the photo of me for the back cover.

For acknowledging the writer in me and for urging me to get onto paper whatever books are in my head, thank you, **Vimala Rodgers**. And thank you for your continued support along the way.

Thank you also to my husband **Talmadge Heath** for always believing in my abilities.

Special thanks to my daughter **Rebecca Stamos** for providing me with the constant anticipation of outings and other days more glamorous and diverse than the ones spent sitting at a computer. You'll never know how valuable and helpful that is to keep me going!

Finally, **Shylo and Chance**, thank you for keeping my blood flowing by getting me out on long daily walks on the Bay no matter how wild the weather.

introduction

This is a teachers' resource book of Bingo games for ESL and EFL classes.

Some of the material, especially much of Section One—Vocabulary Bingo, is quite obvious and will require no more preparation than:

a. deciding exactly which and how many items the students need more exposure to, and what words, sentences, and/or questions will be used to cue them,

b. copying blank *Bingo grids* (from the back of the book) for the students to fill out themselves before the game,

c. providing *markers*, that is, something with which the students can mark their responses on their Bingo grids (dried beans, corn or cut up cardboard), and

d. providing some sort of *prizes* for the winners.

Others require considerably more preparation in the form of:

e. *lessons*, suggestions for which are included in most cases, especially for the more intricate games of Section Two—Grammar Bingo, or

f. *ear-training*, as in the games of Section Three—Phonology Bingo.

Included also with this book, but separate from its binding, is a packet of card-stock pages of *calling cards*, the cards needed by the instructor or other person calling out the items at random for the students to respond to on their Bingo grids.

Prizes? Yes. Even for adults, there is a need to have some sort of prize. Without a prize there is no closure to the game, and it will feel very awkward and anticlimactic to go on and play a new game when someone has just won with no consequence. The least expensive way to go is to buy a big bag of wrapped candies. For instructors who prefer not to give their students sugar, however, small school supply items are also very enthusiastically received, for example brightly colored pencils, pens, or erasers. Suggestions for other prizes particularly appropriate to the game at hand are included in some of the notes in Section Three.

Bingo grids. Each student's Bingo grid has to be different, of course, or theoretically everyone will win at the same time. This means that simply preparing one grid and then making copies of it for each student is not appropriate. There are several options for the preparation of the grids:

> a) **The students can each prepare their own.** Instructions on how to direct this are included with each game or group of games. This takes a bit of class time and, perhaps in the case of literacy students, *too much* time. However, the advantages are that the students get some valuable practice in following directions, they are much more familiar with the location of the items on their grids when they're finished than they would be had they not prepared them themselves, and the instructor has far less preparation to do before class.

> b) **The grids can be prepared on computer** using a number of Bingo software products available.

> c) **The instructor can prepare each grid.** This is not difficult if the class is small and/or the items in the game are few. If the students have severely limited literacy skills, and no computer software is available, it may be the best, or *only*, way to go, to avoid wasting time and frustrating the students *and* the teacher.

A note from the author about spelling:

Due to my commitment to spelling reform, I have spelled the words *through, though and although* with the alternate spellings *thru, tho* and *altho,* respectively, thruout this book except (ironically) where they appear on pages to be duplicated for your students. Please excuse any distraction this may cause during reading.

SECTION ONE
VOCABULARY BINGO

INTRODUCTION

This first section consists of seven chapters full of the more obvious objects of Bingo games: lexical items. It begins with **"Simple Games"** which can be adapted to review and reinforce whatever vocabulary you and your students have encountered in your lessons, dialogs and readings in recent days. It continues with a variety of games to practice *specific* sets of lexical items—**alphabet** (pronunciation and order of the letters), **numbers** (from the simplest lesson for the lowest beginners, to games that cover larger numbers), **days and months** (for calendar practice), **parts of the body** (including the most challenging game for you the teacher!), **personal information** (answering questions and filling out simple forms), and **kinship terms** (including exposure to many common English first names).

CHAPTER 1
SIMPLE GAMES

The three games in this chapter are general games that can be adapted to reinforce and review any vocabulary being presented in ESL classes. The first is best suited only for literacy students, but the other two may be used at any level of ESL.

WORD RECOGNITION
FOR ESL LITERACY STUDENTS

For a simple end-of-the-week Bingo game, select any 9 words (for 3x3 Bingo grids), any 16 words (for 4x4 grids), or any 25 words (for 5x5 grids), depending on the capabilities of your students, from the words you have been using and teaching in your lessons for the week.

SET-UP & PREPARATION: Write the selected items on the chalkboard and review their meanings. Give each student a Bingo grid. Have the students copy one word in each square of their grids *in random order* (so that each grid will be different).

While the students are preparing their Bingo grids, prepare your calling cards by writing each of the words on a different card. (Use some of the blank perforated cards provided or use other cards such as index cards cut into smaller cards). Distribute markers to each student.

PLAY THE GAME: Draw the cards one by one at random and read the words on the cards. Students listen to your words and put a marker on the corresponding words on their grids. The first one to have 3 (for 3x3 grids), 4 (for 4x4 grids), or 5 (for 5x5 grids) squares marked *in a row*, calls out "Bingo!" Have the winner read the words s/he has marked. If all words are words you have indeed called, the winner gets a prize. Everyone clears their grids for a new game. If any words do not match those you have called, play continues until someone else has "Bingo."

If some of the best students in the class are able to pronounce the words comprehensibly (and especially if one or two of them tend to win every time, not giving anyone else a chance), give *them* turns at calling the words in your place. This will free you up to go around and assist students who are having problems with the game.

WORD CUES
FOR ALL ESL LEVELS

For these games, pairs of vocabulary items are taught together, such as two forms of verbs:

go	went
see	saw
feel	felt
fall	fell
fill	filled
want	wanted
	etc.

or pairs of synonyms:

seize	take
enter	come in
eradicate	get rid of
remove	take off
apply	put on
set	put
	etc.

or opposites:

young	old
thick	thin
come	go
fast	slow
	etc.

Write on the blackboard the list of pairs you want to review.

For the Bingo games, students write one word of each pair (*you* specify *which* word, for example, "all the words on this side of the board") into their Bingo grids (for example the past forms) and the corresponding words (the basic forms) are called by the teacher as cues. In other words, for a game of past forms, the word *go* might be called and the students would respond by putting their markers on the word *went*.

Again, the Bingo grids used may be 3x3s, 4x4s or 5x5s, depending on how many pairs of words you have been working on and also depending on the capabilities of the students in your particular class.

SENTENCE COMPLETION
FOR ALL ESL LEVELS

If your class has encountered quite a lot of new vocabulary in a story or something you have been reading with them, this is a fun way to review or reinforce it.

The procedure is the same as for Word Cues. Write a list of words to review on the board and have students copy them in random order into the squares of their grids. Then, instead of a one-word cue as on the previous page, the teacher provides all but the last word of a *sentence*, the last word being the words on the Bingo grids that the students must identify and mark.

The sentences can be definitions, such as

> *A vehicle used to transport food and other cargo in the snow is a*   **sled**.
> *The kind of dog that Eskimos use to pull their sleds is called a*   **husky**.

where two of the words copied into the Bingo grids (and onto the teacher's calling cards) are *sled* and *husky*,

or they may refer to something that transpired in the story, such as:

> *When Martha came home from work, she found a large*   **package**.
> *The marks on the door had been made with a*   **hammer**.

where two of the words copied into the Bingo grids (and onto the teacher's calling cards) are *package* and *hammer*.

To play the game, the teacher reads the beginning of one of the sentences, leaving off the final word, and each student places a marker on the word on her/his Bingo grid which completes the sentence. Again, the first student to correctly mark a complete row gets a prize.

CHAPTER 2

ALPHABET

These games familiarize students with the English alphabet and our pronunciation of the letters. The second game can also drill the *order* of the letters, for students whose alphabetizing skills are weak or non-existent. The set-up and preparation are the same for both games.

LESSON: Practice the pronunciation of the letters by having students repeat them after you. Next, have them spell their names orally as you listen and respond by writing them letter-by-letter on the board. In pairs, have them ask *each other* how to spell their names: "What is your last name? How do you spell it? What is your first name? How do you spell it?" The student who is asking can write the letters on a piece of paper as you did on the board. At some point in the process practice difficult pairs such as b/v, c/z, a/i/e, j/g, k/q, m/n, b/p, t/d, x/s, i/y (depending on which language groups you have in your class).

SET-UP: At this point you probably already have the letters of the alphabet written all over the chalkboard. If not, write them up there now. If you are going to use this game partly for alphabetical order (see Game 2), write the alphabet *in order* for the students.

PREPARATION: Give each student a 5x5 Bingo grid. Point out that there are 26 letters in the English alphabet and only 25 squares on the Bingo grid. Tell them to put *two* of the letters in the center square and only one letter in each of the other squares. Emphasize the importance of *not* writing the letters in order because "this is for Bingo, so everybody needs to have a different order."

If this is not clear, demonstrate how they can write the alphabet out of order in the squares: Hold a Bingo grid up for all to see, or use an overhead projector, and write **A** in any square but the first (upper left-hand corner), **B** in any other but not adjacent to the **A**, **C** in any other but not adjacent to the **B**, and so on, moving around the grid as randomly as you can.

One student's grid may look like this:

E	S	Q	V	C
R	n	A	T	G
H	B	ĐW	K	F
U	L	Z	J	O
m	X	I	P	y

As they prepare their grids, give each student a handful of markers. The calling cards for these games are provided with this book.

GAME 1—*SIMPLE LETTERS*

EXPLAIN THE GAME: (Suggested script:) **I'm going to pronounce the name of one letter. Find on your grid the letter you hear and put a marker on it like this. Only one marker is necessary for the center square. (Only one letter of the two letters is necessary.) When you have 5 marked squares in a row, say "Bingo!" They can be horizontal, like this, or vertical, like this, or diagonal, like this. The first person to say Bingo and is correct is the winner. The second person is—too late.**

PLAY THE GAME: Scramble the 26 calling cards face down, then select one at random and read it.

After giving the students enough time to find the correct letter on their Bingo grids, set the card aside and select another card at random and read it. Continue selecting, reading, and setting aside the calling cards until someone says "Bingo!" If no one says Bingo, but you notice that someone has five marked squares in a row, point this out and coach them to say *Bingo!*

CHECK FOR CORRECT RESPONSES: Go to the potential winner's seat so you can look at the winning grid as s/he reads the five winning squares to you. Check them against the calling cards you have called and set aside. (The instructor or an aide needs to visually check the responses for this game because the students may have marked, for example, the letter *E* when you read *A*, and then read *A* back to you as they look at their *E*, two wrongs sounding to you like a right, but actually making a double wrong, thus defeating the purpose of the game.)

If all five are correct, give the winner a prize. Have everyone clear their grids of markers and begin again. "New game!"

If any of the five squares do not match the items you have called, announce that there is "No Bingo!—Let's continue!" (If someone asks *which one* is not correct, say, "I can't tell you that.")

GAME 2—*QUESTIONS*

Here's where alphabetical order comes in, but other questions can be asked too. (Any questions asked for the game should be asked and practiced beforehand.) Examples:

For the letter **A:**   What's the first letter of the alphabet?   or
What letter comes before *B*?   or
What's the first letter of the name *America*?

For the letter **B**:   What's the second letter of the alphabet?   or

What letter comes before *C*?   or

What letter comes after *A*?   or

What letter comes between *A* and *C*?   or

What's the first letter of the name *Barbara*?

For the letter **C**:   What's the third letter of the alphabet?   or

What letter comes before *D*?   or

What letter comes after *B*?   or

What letter comes between *B* and *D*?   or

What's the first letter of the name *Charles*?

Note that for the letter *C*, the third question is trickier (for some language groups) because it checks *both* the comprehension of the question (requiring knowledge of the order of the alphabet and comprehension of the word *after*) *as well as* the phonological recognition of the letter *B* as opposed to *V*. The second question might not be as interesting if the name of the letter *D* is not phonologically confused with any other letter name by the language groups in your class.

EXPLAIN THE GAME: (Suggested script:) **I'm going to ask a question. Find the correct answer on your paper and put a marker on it like this. Only one marker is necessary for the center square. (Only one letter of the two letters is necessary.) When you have 5 marked squares in a row, say "Bingo!" They can be horizontal, like this, or vertical, like this, or diagonal, like this. The first person to say *Bingo* and is correct is the winner. The second person is—too late.**

PLAY THE GAME: Scramble the 26 calling cards face down; then select one at random and ask a question, as above, which will elicit as an answer the letter you have drawn.

After giving the students enough time to find the correct letter on their Bingo grids, set the card aside and select another card at random and ask a question to elicit it. Continue selecting, asking, and setting aside the calling cards until someone says "Bingo!" If no one says *Bingo*, but you notice that someone has five marked squares in a row, point this out and coach them to say *Bingo!*

CHECK FOR CORRECT RESPONSES: Have the potential winner read the five winning squares to you. Check them against the calling cards you have called and set aside.

If all five are correct, give the winner a prize. Have everyone clear their grids of markers and begin again. "New game!"

If any of the five squares do not match the items you have called, announce that there is "No Bingo!—Let's continue!" (If someone asks *which one* is not correct, tell them "I can't tell you that.")

CHAPTER 3

NUMBERS

Here are six games of varying difficulty for practicing numbers. Use the variations to create your own games in order to fine-tune the difficulty to the level of your class.

The first four games are for very low beginners and literacy students.

GAME 1: 3x3—*NAMES OF NUMBERS, 1-9*

This game simply requires very low beginners or literacy students to recognize the numbers 1 2 3 4 5 6 7 8 9 and their corresponding English words. After introducing the pronunciation of the numbers from one to nine, simply have students copy one digit in each square of a 3x3 Bingo grid in random order.

One student's grid might look like this:

3	9	4
7	2	6
8	1	5

Calling cards for all the games in this chapter are provided with this book.

GAME 2: 3x3—*WORDS FOR NUMBERS, ONE thru NINE*

LESSON: In their notebooks, have the students copy the first nine number words next to the corresponding numerals.

For more practice, give each student nine cards. Have them copy one number word, *without* the corresponding numeral, on each card. Then have them scramble the cards and put them back in numerical order.

For the Bingo game, have them copy the nine numbers as in Game 1, but this time have them write the number *words* instead of the numerals.

One student's grid might look like this:

three	nine	four
seven	two	six
eight	one	five

GAME 3: 4x4—*NAMES OF NUMBERS, 1-20*

A next step in difficulty would be to add the numbers up to 20. Now using 4x4 grids instead of 3x3s, point out that there are 20 numbers and only 16 squares. Therefore when they copy the numbers in random order on their grids, they will have to leave out 4 of them.

One student's grid may look like this (with the numbers 2, 7, 13, 19 omitted):

3	20	10	12
18	9	1	17
4	15	5	11
8	6	14	16

GAME 4: 4x4—*WORDS FOR NUMBERS, ONE thru TWENTY*

Again, an alternative is to have them copy the number *words* instead, as in Game 2.

Games 5 and 6 are for beginners and low intermediate students.

GAME 5: 4x4—*PHONOLOGICAL PROBLEMS WITH NUMBERS*

This game addresses the phonological difficulty many students have recognizing the difference between the pronunciation of the numbers 13 and 30, 14 and 40, 15 and 50, 16 and 60, 17 and 70, 18 and 80, 19 and 90. Since this list consists of only fourteen words and the 4x4 grid has sixteen squares, let's add the numbers 12 and 20 altho this is not such a troublesome pair.

LESSON: Practice distinguishing the sounds of each pair by listing the teens 13, 14, 15, 16, 17, 18, 19 on one side of the chalkboard and the tens 30, 40, 50, 60, 70, 80, 90 on the other.

Point to the numbers as you pronounce the pairs together: 13/30, 14/40, etc., so that students can clearly hear the contrast in pronunciation. Be sure that your pronunciation is loud and clear. Raising your pitch may help. If necessary, exaggerate the differences (stress, final *n*, length of final syllable) until the students catch on to them, but then return to a more normal pronunciation.

Next ask the students to point to the number that you pronounce. Standing between the two lists, but looking out at the class, pronounce one of the numbers of either list. After a few students point to one side of the board or the other (they are *all supposed to* but it may take a few tries to engage the whole class), point to the number you just pronounced.

Repeat several times, pronouncing and having the class point to a different number each time, and selecting as randomly as you can from one list or the other. (Don't be obvious by switching from one list to the other *every* time or by providing them with other cues such as a change in your intonation *only* when you switch lists. The only cue they should be getting is the difference in pronunciation between the two lists.)

PREPARATION: Give each student a 4x4 Bingo grid. Point out that there are 16 numbers on the chalkboard and 16 squares on the Bingo grid. Tell them to copy one number in each square, but not in the same order they see on the board. Emphasize the importance of *not* writing the numbers in order because "this is for Bingo, so everybody needs to have a different order."

If this is not clear, demonstrate how they can write the numbers out of order in the squares: Hold a Bingo grid up for all to see, or use an overhead projector, and write **12** in any square but the first (upper left-hand corner), **13** in any other but not adjacent to **12**, **14** in any other but not adjacent to the **13**, and so on, moving around the grid as randomly as you can.

As they prepare their grids, give each student a handful of markers.

EXPLAIN THE GAME: (Suggested script:) **I'm going to pronounce the name of one number. Look at your grid to find the number you hear and put a marker on it like this. When you have 4 marked squares in a row, say "Bingo!" They can be horizontal, like this, or vertical, like this, or diagonal, like this. The first person to say *Bingo* and is correct is the winner. The second person is——too late.**

PLAY THE GAME: Scramble the 16 calling cards, provided with this book, face down, then select one at random and read it.

After giving the students enough time to find the correct number on their Bingo grids, set the card aside and select another card at random and read it. Continue selecting, reading, and setting aside the calling cards until someone says "Bingo!" If no one says

Bingo, but you notice that someone has four marked squares in a row, point this out and coach them to say *Bingo!*

Note: For this game, do *not* continue selecting calling cards *completely* at random. It's a good idea to avoid calling both items of a contrasting pair, if possible. If, for example, 14 has already been drawn, then if 40 comes up, set it aside *without* calling it until one of each contrasting pair has been drawn. If no one achieves Bingo after these first 8 (one of each pair) *then* go back and call the others until someone says Bingo. Why? Whenever both 14 and 40 are called, the students may mark 14 for 40 and vice versa, thereby possibly getting Bingo without having heard either item correctly. This, of course, defeats the whole purpose of the game.

CHECK FOR CORRECT RESPONSES:

Go to the potential winner's seat so you can look at the winning grid as s/he reads the four winning squares to you. Check them against the calling cards you have called and set aside. (The instructor or an aide needs to visually check the responses for this game because the student may have marked, for example, the number **30** when you read **13**, and then read **13** back to you as they look at their **30**, two wrongs sounding to you like a right, but actually making a double wrong, thus defeating the purpose of the game.)

If all four are correct, give the winner a prize. Have everyone clear their grids of markers and begin again. "New game!"

If any of the four squares do not match the items you have called, announce that there is "No Bingo!—Let's continue!" (If someone asks which one is not correct, answer "I can't tell you that.")

GAME 6: *LARGER NUMBERS*

LESSON: For spelling practice, and to learn the English system of words for numbers, have the students write the numbers on the worksheets on the following pages. (Altho most students enjoy these worksheets, they're pretty dry, so try to limit the assignment to one or two pages per day.)

(Permission granted to reproduce the following 5 pages for ESL classroom use.)

WORDS FOR NUMBERS—1-60

1 one	21 twenty-one	41 _____
2 two	22 twenty-two	42 _____
3 three	23 _____	43 _____
4 four	24 _____	44 _____
5 five	25 _____	45 _____
6 six	26 _____	46 _____
7 seven	27 _____	47 _____
8 eight	28 _____	48 _____
9 nine	29 _____	49 _____
10 ten	30 thirty	50 fifty
11 eleven	31 thirty-one	51 _____
12 twelve	32 _____	52 _____
13 thirteen	33 _____	53 _____
14 fourteen	34 _____	54 _____
15 fifteen	35 _____	55 _____
16 sixteen	36 _____	56 _____
17 seventeen	37 _____	57 _____
18 eighteen	38 _____	58 _____
19 nineteen	39 _____	59 _____
20 twenty	40 forty	60 sixty

WORDS FOR NUMBERS—61-100

60	sixty	80	eighty	

60   sixty

61 _____

62 _____

63 _____

64 _____

65 _____

66 _____

67 _____

68 _____

69 _____

70   seventy

71 _____

72 _____

73 _____

74 _____

75 _____

76 _____

77 _____

78 _____

79 _____

80   eighty

80   eighty

81 _____

82 _____

83 _____

84 _____

85 _____

86 _____

87 _____

88 _____

89 _____

90   ninety

91 _____

92 _____

93 _____

94 _____

95 _____

96 _____

97 _____

98 _____

99 _____

100   one hundred

WORDS FOR NUMBERS—100-20,000

1 one	100	one hundred	1000	one thousand
2 two	200	____	2000	____
3 three	300	____	3000	____
4 four	400	____	4000	____
5 five	500	____	5000	____
6 six	600	____	6000	____
7 seven	700	____	7000	____
8 eight	800	____	8000	____
9 nine	900	____	9000	____
10 ten	110	one hundred ten	10,000	____
11 eleven	211	____	11,000	____
12 twelve	312	____	12,000	____
13 thirteen	413	____	13,000	____
14 fourteen	514	____	14,000	____
15 fifteen	615	____	15,000	____
16 sixteen	716	____	16,000	____
17 seventeen	817	____	17,000	____
18 eighteen	918	____	18,000	____
19 nineteen	1100	eleven hundred	19,000	____
20 twenty	1219	____	20,000	____

WORDS FOR NUMBERS—22,000-610,000

22,000	twenty-two thousand
33,000	_____
44,000	_____
55,000	_____
66,000	_____
77,000	_____
88,000	_____
99,000	_____
100,000	one hundred thousand
111,000	_____
112,000	_____
200,000	_____
203,000	_____
300,000	_____
342,000	_____
400,000	_____
478,000	_____
500,000	_____
501,000	_____
600,000	_____
610,000	_____

WORDS FOR NUMBERS—700,000-21,000,000,000

700,000   _____

719,000   _____

800,000   _____

836,000   _____

900,000   _____

982,000   _____

999,999   _____

_____

1,000,000   one million

2,000,000   _____

5,000,000   _____

8,000,000   _____

10,000,000   _____

27,000,000   _____

86,000,000   _____

100,000,000   _____

579,000,000   _____

999,000,000   _____

1,000,000,000   one billion

13,000,000,000   _____

21,000,000,000   _____

NUMBER DICTATION: As a follow-up to each of these written pages, have the students write some of the numbers (or similar numbers) of the page just finished, in response to your dictation of one number at a time. Emphasize that you want them to write *only the number, not the words for the numbers*, during the dictation part of this exercise.

To check their work, after each 5 or 6 dictated numbers, have them call out the numbers of the dictation as you write them in a column on the board. They can then check and correct their own papers.

Next, draw a line under each number, extending the line way beyond the number itself, and ask them to now write the word for the number, to practice the spelling of the words. After giving them adequate time for this, write the words on the board, or have student volunteers write them so that the students can correct their own work.

Suggested dictation for page 18:

12 _____
20 _____
8 _____
11 _____
60 _____
19 _____

for page 19:

18 _____
50 _____
30 _____
14 _____
90 _____
16 _____
70 _____

Suggested dictation for page 20:

900 _____
6000 _____
415 _____
888 _____
72 _____
12,000 _____
1200 *Twelve hundred*

for page 21:

236,000 _____
504,000 _____
911,000 _____
27,000 _____
2700 _____

etc.

SET-UP: Write the following 41 numbers on the chalkboard:

13	14	15	16	17	18	19
30	40	50	60	70	80	90
107	108	109	110	111	112	113
700	800	900		1100	1200	1300
1007	1008	1009	1010	1011	1012	1013
7000	8000	9000	10,000	11,000	12,000	13,000

PREPARATION: Give each student a 5x5 Bingo grid. Show them that there are only 25 squares on their Bingo grids but 41 numbers on the chalkboard. Tell them to copy only 25 of the 41 numbers into the 25 squares of the Bingo grid.

It's important not to copy them in order, so that each person will have a *different* order.

If this is not clear, demonstrate how they can write the numbers out of order in the squares as in Game 5.

One student's grid may look like the one below.

As they prepare their grids, give each student a handful of markers.

Explain and play the game as in Game 5. Calling cards are provided.

107	1010	60	800	19
50	700	108	13	12,000
900	14	1011	110	70
1012	111	40	15	1100
18	16	1200	109	30

CHAPTER 4
DAYS & MONTHS

LESSON: Write the following questions on the board. Have the students copy the questions and write the short answers if they know them:
(or distribute copies of the questions for the students to answer.)

1. What day is today?
2. What day was yesterday?
3. What was the day before yesterday?
4. What day is tomorrow?
5. What is the day after tomorrow?
6. What day is before [fill in answer to #3]?
7. What day is after [fill in answer to #5]?

After most students have had time to copy and answer the questions, go over the answers together, writing them on the board, pointing out the days on a calendar as you go, and encouraging students to correct their own papers.

Practice the correct pronunciation of the questions and answers.

Pair practice: Have the students ask each other the questions.

Follow the same procedures with the following questions, perhaps in a different class session:

1. What month is this?
2. What month is next month?
3. What's the month after next?
4. What was last month?
5. What was the month before last?
6. What month is before [fill in answer to #5]?
7. What month is after [fill in answer to #3]?
8. What month is between [fill in answer to #6 and two months earlier, for example, October and August]?
9. What month is between [fill in answer to #7 and two months later, for example, April and June]?
10. What month is after [fill in last month in question #9, June in our example]?

SET-UP: On the board, write the seven names of the days of the week and the twelve names of the months of the year. If the above exercises are still on the board, the names are already there and need only to be circled, or everything else erased around them.

PREPARATION: Give each student a 4x4 Bingo grid. Show them that there are 16 squares on their Bingo grids and 19 names on the chalkboard (7 days + 12 months). Tell them to copy the names of only 16 of the 19 days and months into the 16 squares of the Bingo grid.

It's important not to copy them in order, so that each person will have a *different* order.

If this is not understood, go thru several of the names together, allowing time for everyone to copy each item (in *any* square) before going on to the next. One student's grid may look like this (with January, June, and Saturday left out):

April	Monday	February	Tuesday
Friday	March	Sunday	December
October	Wednesday	August	May
July	September	Thursday	November

As the students prepare their Bingo grids, you can hand out bingo markers to each student. The calling cards for this game are provided with this book.

EXPLAIN THE GAME: (Suggested script:) **I'm going to ask a question. For example, "What was last month?" or "What's the second month of the year?"** [Use only questions familiar to the students from previous practice.] **Don't *say* anything! Just put a marker on the correct answer on your paper. When you have 4 squares in a row with markers, say, "Bingo!" They can be horizontal, like this, or vertical, like this, or diagonal, like this. The first person to say *Bingo* and is correct is the winner. The second person is— too late!**

Repeat any of this that is not clear. Try as many examples as necessary to check everyone's comprehension of the language as well as the procedures.

PLAY THE GAME: Scramble the 19 calling cards face down, then select one at random and ask any comprehensible question which elicits the response on that card.

After giving the students enough time to find the correct answer on their Bingo grids, set the card aside and select another card at random and ask a question.

Continue selecting, asking, and setting aside the calling cards until someone says "Bingo!" If no one says *Bingo*, but you notice that someone has three marked squares in a row, point this out and coach them to say *Bingo!*

CHECK FOR CORRECT RESPONSES: Have the potential winner read the four winning squares to you. Check them against the calling cards you have called and set aside. If all four squares are correct, give the winner a prize. Have everyone clear their grids of markers and begin again. "New game!"

If the four squares do not match the items you have called, announce that there is "No Bingo!—Let's continue!"

Note: Do not reveal *which* of their answers is not correct because then other students will begin rearranging their markers according to this information and at least one person, but probably several, will come up a winner without having known the answers on their own, defeating the whole purpose of the exercise.

So make a point of listening to all four of the potential winner's answers before declaring that there is "No Bingo!" And when the students ask, "Which one?" say that you can't tell them that.

CHAPTER 5

PARTS OF THE BODY

This chapter uses TPR to learn, acquire and practice the names of body parts in English. Then a variety of Bingo games can be used to reinforce them.

LESSON: Tell the students:

> Touch your nose. [while you touch your own nose]
> Touch your chin. [while you touch your own chin]
>   etc.

Give them only a few new words at a time before you go back and repeat the same commands *without* modeling the action, in order to check their comprehension. Then repeat each command many *more* times, *even after it is clear that the students understand everything.* This is for reinforcement, practice and comprehensible input.

Add not only more body parts, but also several different verbs:

> **Scratch** your neck, nose, back, leg.
> **Don't scratch** your eyes!
> **Move** your head, your eyes, your arms, hands, fingers, lips.
> **Rub** your neck, your arm, your knee, your back.

Only when students are responding appropriately and easily to the commands (probably after several class sessions, depending on how fast they are picking it up). should you ask them to try to pronounce the words themselves. The next step is for you to have them give *you* the commands. Finally, have them practice in pairs, with the students telling *each other* what to do.

Once their pronunciation sounds fairly good (*or alternatively*, as soon as you see them trying to write down what they're hearing, and *butchering* the spelling), provide them with a list of the words you are using, body parts and verbs. You may want to write the full imperative sentences on the board like this:

| Don't | Touch
scratch
cover
move
rub | your | head
hair
face
eyes
ear
nose
mouth
Tongue
Tooth, Teeth
chin
neck
back
butt
stomach | shoulder
arm
elbow
wrist
hand
fingers
leg
knee
ankle
foot, feet
toes |

Follow this with more oral practice and a **dictation** of the full sentences, to practice listening and spelling.

A further step you may want to take is to use these actions to introduce or practice the **present continuous** tense:

> Gina, scratch your shoulder.
> Everybody, look at Gina. What is she doing?
> Yes, she's **scratching** her shoulder.
> Is she scratching her nose? No, she's **not scratching** her nose.
>   etc.

This may also be followed with a **dictation** of complete questions and answers.

Note about dictations: Allow low beginners or less literate students to refer to the written list of words during the dictation so that they will be practicing the spellings *correctly*. Some students may have to copy every word; that's all right; for them the exercise is more a decode-and-copy exercise than a dictation, but they will learn a lot about spelling and writing from it, and at the same time gain confidence in their ability to keep up.

GAME 1: FOR LITERACY STUDENTS

Give each student a 5x5 Bingo grid and have them copy the names of 25 body parts into the 25 squares *in random order*. (If you object to using the word *butt*, substitute something else.)

Scramble the 25 provided calling cards face down. Draw one at random and read the word on it.

GAME 2: *SILENT BINGO* FOR LITERACY AND LOW BEGINNERS

Use the same Bingo grids as in Game 1, but instead of *reading* the words on the cards, point to or touch the part of the body named on the card you draw. You may use your own body, or, if this makes you uncomfortable, use a large picture of a person to point to.

Note: In order to be very clear each time you are showing a new item, signal each one with a verbal cue as well, such as *number 1, number 2*, etc., or "Here's the next one, ready? Look, everybody."

Another way to do this is to use one of the verbs used in the practice. For example, if the card drawn says *back,* scratch your back as you say, "Look: I'm scratching my [pause]."

GAME 3: *TPR BINGO* FOR ALL BEGINNING LEVELS

OK, finally a Bingo game that presents a challenge to you the teacher! This is guaranteed to be much less boring to you than any other Bingo game you've ever called.

It's similar to the last suggestion in Game 2, but when you draw the card *chest,* instead of *only* scratching your chest as you say "I'm scratching my [pause]," this time you *scratch your chest* with one hand, and *at the same time* do another action with your other hand, such as *covering your eyes.* So it's a little like a multiple choice exercise, where the students must recognize not only the noun (the body part indicated) but also the verb, distinguishing between the two verbs being performed.

This will be very entertaining to the students because you will be fairly comical-looking doing two of these actions at a time. Hopefully you're adventurous enough to try it!

Note: Play Games 1 and 2 a few times as a warm-up for Game 3.

CHAPTER 6
PERSONAL INFORMATION
FOR VERY LOW BEGINNERS OR LITERACY STUDENTS:

GAME 1: *ANSWERING QUESTIONS*

LESSON & SET-UP: Ask *one* student the following questions and write his or her answers on the board:

1. **What's your last name? How do you spell it?** (Write it out on the board as s/he spells it.)

2. **What's your first name? How do you spell it?** (Write it out on the board as s/he spells it.)

3. **What's your address?** (Write the complete address on the board as if addressing an envelope, that is, number and street on one line; city, state and zip code directly under it.)

4. **What's your phone number?** (Write only the number on the board.)

5. **Where are you from?** (Write only the name of the country, anywhere on the board.)

6. **How old are you?** (Hopefully you've selected a student you can comfortably ask this question!)

7. **What is your birth date (or date of birth)?** (Write only the birth date—no complete sentences here.)

PRACTICE: With one student's answers to these 7 questions on the board, ask the whole class the following questions, pointing out the answers on the board when the group comes up with them:

1. What's Ari's last name? (spelling is not necessary now.)

2. What's his first name?

3. What's his city?

4. What's his street?

5. What's his zip code?

6. What's his phone number?

7. Where is he from?

8. How old is he?

9. What is his birth date (or date of birth?)

Repeat these questions until all students can answer correctly or at least point to the correct answer on the board.

PREPARATION: Draw a circle or rectangle around each answer as you ask the practice questions (above) once more. The board will now look something like this:

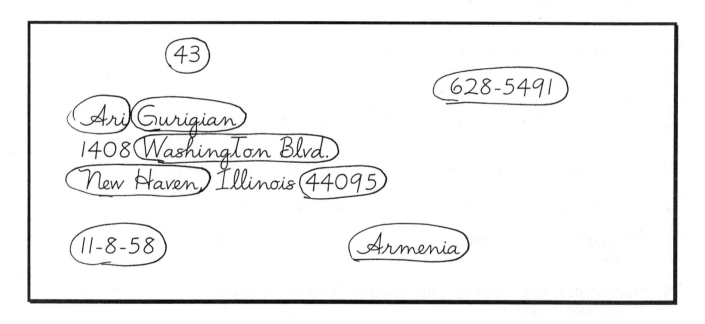

Distribute the Bingo grids and have the students copy the contents of each of the nine circles or rectangles on the board into each of the nine squares on their Bingo grids. Urge them not to copy them in the same order that they see on the board. Remind them that this is Bingo and so every grid needs to be different. If this is difficult to convey, go thru each of the nine items together, giving time for everyone to copy each item (in *any* square) before going on to the next.

One student's grid may look like this:

628-5491	11/8/58	Armenia
43	Guregian	44095
Ari	Washington Blvd.	New Haven

As the students prepare their Bingo grids, you can prepare your calling cards. Copy the contents of each of the nine circles or rectangles onto a separate card (use some of the blank perforated cards provided or use other cards such as index cards cut into smaller cards).

Hand out Bingo markers to each student.

EXPLAIN THE GAME: (Suggested script:) **I'm going to ask a question, for example, "What's Ari's phone number?" Don't *say* anything! Just put a marker on the correct square on your paper. When you have three squares in a row with markers, say, "Bingo!" They can be horizontal, like this, or vertical, like this, or diagonal, like this. The first person to say *Bingo* and is correct is the winner. The second person is—too late!**

Repeat any of this that is not clear. Try as many examples as necessary to check everyone's comprehension of the language as well as the procedures.

PLAY THE GAME: Scramble the nine calling cards face down, then select one at random and ask the question which elicits the response on that card. (For example, if you select *Washington Blvd.*, ask "What's Ari's street?" or "What street does Ari live on?")

After giving the students enough time to find the correct answer on their Bingo grids, set the card aside and select another card at random and ask the corresponding question. (Use the student's name for the first question and the possessive adjective *his* or *her* for subsequent questions.)

Continue selecting, asking, and setting aside the calling cards until someone says "Bingo!" If no one says *Bingo*, but you notice that someone has three marked squares in a row, point this out and coach them to say *Bingo*!

CHECK FOR CORRECT RESPONSES: Have the potential winner read the three winning squares to you. Check them against the calling cards you have called and set aside.

If all three are correct, give the winner a prize. Have everyone clear their grids of markers and begin again. "New game!"

If the three squares do not match the items you have called, announce that there is "No Bingo!—Let's continue!"

VARIATIONS

For very slow or illiterate students, limit yourselves to only 3 of the questions in the Lesson and Practice on pages 33-34. Then ask *three different students* each of the three questions, writing their answers on the board, or having them write their answers on the board themselves (if their renderings will be clear enough for the others to copy on their Bingo grids).

In subsequent sessions, groups of three other questions can be used. Finally, the original 9-item game can be used to review all nine questions.

For 4x4 Bingo grids, eliminate one of the questions in the Lesson on page 33 and its corresponding question in the Practice (pages 33-34), and ask *two* students each of the 8 questions remaining, resulting in 16 answers instead of only nine. Or ask only *four* of the questions of *four* different students, being careful to select four people whose answers are *all different*!

Note: If *all* your students have the same information for one or more of the items, substitute different items. Some suggestions: occupation, middle name or initial, initials, apartment number.

GAME 2: *FILLING IN A FORM*

This Bingo game itemizes and drills the basic personal information requested on a typical form to familiarize very beginning or illiterate students with each of these items.

LESSON: Have the students fill in a simple form similar to the one on page 39 (permission granted to duplicate pages 39-40 for ESL classroom use) before and/or after playing this Bingo game. When they're finished, distribute copies of the interview questions on page 40. Practice pronouncing the questions correctly. Distribute a *second* copy of the blank form to each student. Instruct them to fill in the form with another student's information as they ask each other the interview questions. ("Don't fill in *your* information again—you already did that! Now put in the *other* person's information.")

SET-UP & PRACTICE: Same as for Game 1 on pages 33-34.

PREPARATION: Write on the board the following nine items: *last name, first name, city, street, zip code, phone number, age, birth date, country.* Give each student a Bingo grid. Have the students copy one of the items into each of the nine squares on their Bingo grids. Urge them not to copy them in the same order that they see on the board. Remind them that this is Bingo and so every grid needs to be different. If this is difficult to convey, go thru each of the nine items together, allowing time for everyone to copy each item (in *any* square) before going on to the next.

One student's grid may look like this:

first name	birth date	zip code
street	phone	city
age	country	last name

EXPLAIN THE GAME: (Suggested script:) **I'm going to point to one of [Ari's] answers on the board and ask a question, for example, (pointing to Ari's phone number) "What's this?" (or "This is Ari's _____."** [Wait for students to complete your sentence.]) **Don't *say* anything! Just put a marker on the correct square on your grid, like this. When you have three squares in a row with markers, say, "Bingo!" They can be horizontal, like this, or vertical, like this, or diagonal, like this. The first person to say *Bingo* and is correct is the winner. The second person is—too late.**

PLAY THE GAME: Scramble the nine calling cards provided face down, then select one at random and ask the question which elicits the response on that card. (For example, if you select *first name*, as you point to Ari's first name on the board, ask, "What's this?" or say, "This is Ari's _____.")

After giving the students enough time to find the correct answer on their Bingo grids, set the card aside and select another card at random and ask the corresponding question. (Use the student's name for the first question and the possessive adjective *his* or *her* for subsequent questions.)

Continue selecting, asking, and setting aside the calling cards until someone says "Bingo!" If no one says *Bingo*, but you notice that someone has three marked squares in a row, point this out and coach them to say *Bingo!*

CHECK FOR CORRECT RESPONSES: Have the potential winner read the three winning squares to you. Check them against the calling cards you have called and set aside.

If all three are correct, give the winner a prize. Have everyone clear their grids of markers and begin again. "New game!"

If the three squares do not match the items you have called, announce that there is "No Bingo!—Let's continue!"

APPLICATION FORM
PRACTICE

NAME: _____

              last   first   middle initial

ADDRESS: _____

              number   street

CITY: _____ STATE: _____

ZIP: _____ CROSS STREET: _____

PHONE: ___(_____)_____ — _____ SEX: _____

         area code

AGE: _____ BIRTH DATE: _____/____/_____

                                 mo   day   yr

COUNTRY: _____

SOCIAL SECURITY NUMBER: _____ — _____ — _____

INTERVIEW

1. What's your last name?

2. How do you spell it?

3. What's your first name?

4. How do you spell it?

5. What's your address?

6. What's your cross street?

7. What's your zip code?

8. What's your phone number?

9. How old are you?

10. What's your birth date?

11. Where are you from?

12. What's your social security number?

GAME 3: *SHAPES & PREPOSITIONS*

If your students need more practice with the vocabulary in the previous two games, try this game which adds some more basic vocabulary: basic shapes *circle, square, triangle, rectangle,* and prepositions *above, below, between, in.* Students will make progress by learning something new while reviewing the material already presented.

LESSON: Draw a circle on the chalkboard and label it *circle.* Also draw a square, a rectangle and a triangle, pointing out the differences, and label each of these. The students will probably copy these shapes and words in their notebooks and should be encouraged to do so.

Erase the board. Ask for a volunteer to come to the front of the class and draw a square on the board. (She may try drawing a very small square. Have her draw a square that's big enough to write her first name in legibly.) When the square is successfully drawn, ask the student to write her

> *first name **in** the square,*
> *last name **above** the square,*
> *phone number **below** the square.*

Now ask her to draw a small square next to the big square (or you can draw the small square yourself.) Ask her to write the

> name of her *country **between*** the two squares (or
> between the big square and the small square.)

Ask a second volunteer to come up and draw a circle. Once the circle is there, ask him to write his

> *first name **below** the circle,*
> *last name **in** the circle,*
> *phone number **between** the square and the circle,*
> *birth date **above** the circle.*

Ask a third volunteer to come up and draw a triangle. Once the triangle is there, ask him to write his

> *first name **above** the triangle,*
> *address **in** the triangle,*
> *zip code **between** the triangle and the circle,*
> *age **below** the triangle.*

Ask a fourth volunteer to come up and draw a rectangle. Once the rectangle is there, ask her to write her

> *last name above* the rectangle,
> *address below* the rectangle,
> *birth date between* the triangle and the rectangle,
> *age in* the rectangle.

Next ask the class:

> **What's** *in the square*? That's right, *Sara's first name* is in the square. (point to it)
> **What's** *in the circle*?
> **What's** *between the triangle and the circle*?
>   etc.

Now use a different question form:

> **Where is** Sara's *first name*? That's right, *in the square.*
> **Where's** Ivan's phone number?
>   etc.

There may be only a few students who are ready to try to pronounce all these things. That's fine, just allow the rest to listen. They will be learning just as much in their silence as their noisier, more adventurous classmates who are coming up with the answers.

SET-UP: When you are sure that everyone is at least following this, even if not all answering correctly, write a list of the items the students have written on the board; for example:

Sara's first name	Chen's first name
Sara's last name	Chen's address
Sara's phone number	Chen's zip code
Sara's country	Chen's age
Ivan's first name	Ana's last name
Ivan's last name	Ana's address
Ivan's phone number	Ana's birth date
Ivan's birth date	Ana's age

If you'd like to explain the -'s in these phrases, try it, but at this level just being exposed to it is probably enough. The students will deduce the meaning at some level, if not explicitly at this point.

PREPARATION: Give each student a 4x4 Bingo grid. Point out that there are 16 phrases in the list that you have just written on the chalkboard and 16 squares on the Bingo grid.

Have them copy one phrase into each square, *but not in the same order as you have written them on the board!* This is Bingo and everyone needs a different board.

If this is difficult to convey, point to each item, one at a time, giving everyone enough time to copy it in a *different* square before going on to the next. Check around the room each time to see where students are writing the items until the students are convinced not to write the items in the same order.

While the students are writing the 16 items on their Bingo grids, you can write them on 16 of the blank cards that came with this book (or cut up index cards for this purpose).

EXPLAIN THE GAME: (Suggested script:) **I'm going to ask a question, for example,** *What's between the square and the circle?* (The shapes and the student volunteer's personal information are still up there on the chalkboard in front of everyone.) **The answer is** *Ivan's phone number* (point to where Ivan's phone number is, between the square and the circle). **Don't answer the question! Find the correct answer on your grid and put a marker on it. When you have 4 marked squares in a row, say** *Bingo!* **They can be horizontal, like this, or vertical, like this, or diagonal, like this. The first person to say** *Bingo* **and is correct is the winner. The second person is—too late.**

PLAY THE GAME: Scramble the 16 calling cards face down, then select one at random and ask the question which elicits the response on that card. (For example, if you select *Ana's age*, ask "What's in the rectangle?")

After giving the students enough time to find the correct answer on their Bingo grids, set the card aside and select another card at random and ask the corresponding question.

Continue selecting, asking, and setting aside the calling cards until someone says "Bingo!" If no one says *Bingo*, but you notice that someone has four marked squares in a row, point this out and coach them to say *Bingo!*

CHECK FOR CORRECT RESPONSES: Have the potential winner read the four winning squares to you. Check them against the calling cards you have called and set aside. If all four are correct, give the winner a prize. Have everyone clear their grids of markers and begin again. "New game!"

If the four squares do not match the items you have called, announce that there is "No Bingo!—Let's continue!"

CHAPTER 7

KINSHIP TERMS

This lesson and game cover all the English kinship terms except step-family members (which can easily be added if desired.)

LESSON: Begin by drawing two very simple faces on the chalkboard, side by side, and then introducing them as Grace and Henry—write the names under the faces. Tell the students that **Grace and Henry are married and have two children, a son named Sam and a daughter named Christine.** While you are saying this, draw two more faces, below the first two, and label them *Sam* and *Christine.*

Now ask the students to **look at Sam** (point to your drawing of him) and tell you **the name of his *mother*** (to see if they are following you.) **That's right, her name is Grace. And what's his *father*'s name? Right, Henry. And who is his *sister*? Right, Christine.**

Now have them look at Christine. **Grace is her *mother*, and Henry is her _____** (wait for the students to complete this). **That's right, her *father*. And Sam is her _____. Good, Sam is her *brother*.**

What about for Henry? Who is Christine? That's right; Christine is his *daughter*. And who is Sam? That's right; Sam is his *son*. And Grace is his _____. Right! His *wife*.

Now look at Grace. Who is Henry? Good, Henry is her *husband*. And who are Sam and Christine? (tricky question—speakers of some languages will say *sons*.) **No, Christine is a woman, so she's not a *son*, she's a *daughter*, but what do we call both of them together? Sam and Christine are her *children*.**

Go thru everything again, several times if necessary, until everyone in the class can respond correctly. Then go on with the rest of the family:

OK, well, Christine is married to Ted (draw Ted next to Christine and label him, so that Christine is now between Ted and Sam) **and they have a little boy named Tony** (draw a small face directly under Ted and Christine and label it *Tony*.)

Sam is married, too. He's married to Barbara. (Draw and label Barbara on the other side of Sam from Christine.) **They have a little baby girl and her name is Sally.** (Draw a small face directly under Sam and Barbara and label it *Sally*.)

The chalkboard will finally look something like this:

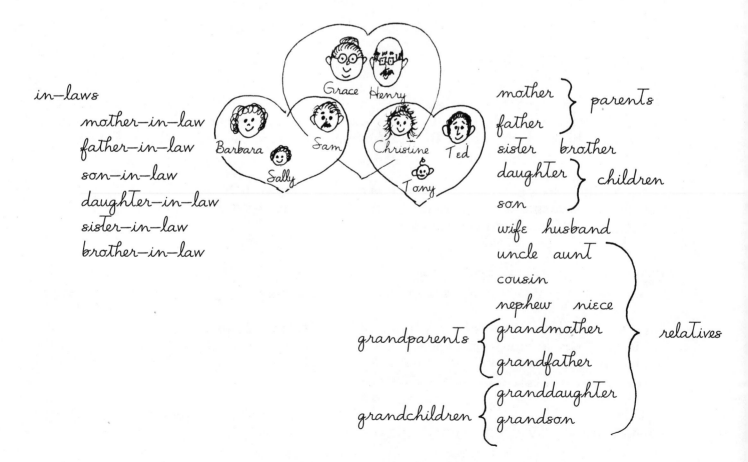

Drawing tips:

1. It's important to make clear the gender of each family member, so draw long hair and/or earrings or bows or *something* to represent females, and short hair and/or some sort of facial hair on all males except the baby Tony.

2. It's also helpful for the first two faces to look a little older. Eyeglasses can do the trick.

3. To clarify the relationships, draw a heart around each of the three family units (see illustration) so that Grace, Henry and their two children are in one heart (draw it as you say they're *married)* and Sam, Barbara and Sally are in another overlapping heart, and Christine, Ted and Tony are in the third heart.

Now proceed thru each person in the illustration, eliciting and/or teaching the kinship terms needed for each relationship, as above. When you feel the students are ready to see the words written, list them on the chalkboard as you come to them, as in the illustration at the bottom of page 46.

More examples:

Now look at Christine again:

Who is Grace?	(her *mother*)
Who is Henry?	(her *father*)
Who are Grace and Henry together?	(her *parents*)
Who is Ted?	(her *husband*)
Who is Tony?	(her *son*)
Who is Sam?	(her *brother*)
Who is Sally?	(her *niece*)
Who is Barbara?	(her *sister-in-law*)

Look at Grace again:

Who is Henry?	(her *husband*)
Who is Christine?	(her *daughter*)
Who is Ted?	(her *son-in-law*)
Who is Sam?	(her *son*)
Who is Barbara?	(her *daughter-in-law*)
Who is Tony?	(her *grandson*)
Who is Sally?	(her *granddaughter*)
Who are Tony and Sally together?	(her *grandchildren*)

Look at Ted:

Who is Henry?	(his *father-in-law*)
Who is Grace?	(his *mother-in-law*)
Who is Christine?	(his *wife*)
Who is Sam?	(his *brother-in-law*)
Who is Barbara?	(sorry, we don't have a word for this; she's his *wife's sister-in-law*)
Who is Tony?	(his *son*)
Who is Sally?	(his *niece*)

Look at Sam and Barbara:

Who is Tony?	(their *nephew*)
Who is Sally?	(their *daughter*)

Look at Tony:

Who is Sally?	(his *cousin*)
Who is Barbara?	(his *aunt*)
Who is Sam ?	(his *uncle*)
Who is Grace?	(his *grandmother*)
Who is Henry?	(his *grandfather*)
Who are Grace and Henry together?	(his *grandparents*)
Who are Grace, Henry, Sam, Barbara, and Sally together?	(his *relatives*)

etcetera!

Give the students copies of the illustration of a different family on the next page (permission granted to duplicate pages 49-50 for ESL classroom use). Have them complete the exercise right away, or for homework, or in the next class session.

For very low-level or literacy students you may need to repeat this lesson several times, in different class sessions, to help the students acquire all these terms, *before* they try the written exercise. Each time you repeat the lesson, use different *typical* names for the family members. This is an excellent way for students to become familiar with frequently used first names in English. (See page 51 for a list of names.)

If writing practice is what your students need more of, create more exercises similar to the one on the next two pages (which you have permission to duplicate for ESL classroom use), changing the names each time, as in the previous paragraph. Have slightly more advanced students answer with *complete sentences* instead of providing them with fill-in-the-blank completions.

FAMILY

Part 1   **Look at Amy:**

1. Who is Julie?   Julie is her ___*mother.*___

2. Who is Ben?   Ben is her _____

3. Who are Sarah and Ben?   They are her _____

4. Who is Billy?   He is her _____

5. Who is Carol?   She is her _____

Part 2   **Look at Nick:**

1. Who is Tom?   Tom is his _____

2. Who is Ben?   Ben is his _____

3. Who is Amy?   She is his _____

4. Who is Billy?   He is his _____

5. Who is Carol?   She is his _____

Part 3   **Look at Sarah:**

1. Who is Julie?   Julie is her _____

2. Who is Ben?   Ben is her _____

3. Who are Amy and Billy? They are her _____

4. Who is Nick?   He is her _____

5. Who is Carol?   She is her _____

Part 4   **Look at Billy:**

1. Who is Tom?   Tom is his _____

2. Who is Sarah?   She is his _____

3. Who is Julie?   She is his _____

4. Who are Carol and
                  Nick?   They are his _____

5. Who are Amy, Julie,
   Tom, Sarah and Ben?   They are his _____

Part 5   **Look at Julie:**

1. Who is Sarah?   Sarah is her _____

2. Who is Tom?   Tom is her _____

3. Who is Ben?   He is her _____

4. Who is Billy?   He is her _____

5. Who is Carol?   She is her _____

In case your mind goes blank as you get ready to name the family members in additional practice sessions, here is a list of simple, typical first names to use:

Rob, Bob, Allen, Ken, Doug, Chris, Frank, Ron, Richard, Dick, Dan, Dave, Mike, Mark, Steve, John, Jack, Jake, Don, Peter, Jim, Kevin, Charley, Chuck, Jeff, Phil, Lenny, Greg, Ed, Harry, Andy, Dennis, James, Will, Roger, Joe, Burt, Paul, Randy, Wayne, Russ, Ross, Todd, Scott, Jason, Alex, Glen, Keith, Gene, Gary, Larry, Ernie, Archie, Eric, Tim,

Anne, Betty, Rebecca, Margie, Ruth, Betsy, Eliza, Lucy, Joan, Kate, Janet, Debra, Ellen, Joyce, Linda, Helen, Kathy, Pamela, Karen, Lisa, Alice, Elaine, Holly, Shirley, Patricia, Brenda, Connie, Jane, Laurie, Denise, Marcia, Francey, Donna, Judy, Vicky, Robin, Peggy, Louise, Thelma, Susan, Diane, Emily, Hillary, Eve, Cindy, Nancy, Jennifer, Rachel, Jean, Doris, Beverly, Sharon, Sandra, Mary, Megan.

BINGO GAME

SET-UP: Introduce one more new family, with new names, in an illustration like the ones on pages 46 and 49. Review some of the questions you have been practicing, pointing out the faces and relationships in the new illustration.

PREPARATION: Give each student a 5x5 Bingo grid in which the center square is marked **FREE.** Have them copy the following 24 words, one in each square, *in random order:*

wife	husband	
sister	brother	
parents	children	
grandparents	grandmother	grandfather
grandchildren	grandson	granddaughter

relatives   aunt   uncle   cousin   niece nephew

mother-in-law	father-in-law
daughter-in-law	son-in-law
sister-in-law	brother-in-law

EXPLAIN THE GAME: (Suggested script:) **I'm going to ask you a question, for example, "Look at Arthur. Who is Hillary?" Don't say anything! Put a marker on the correct answer like this. When you have 5 squares marked in one row, say, "Bingo!" They can be horizontal, like this, or vertical, like this, or diagonal, like this. The first person to say Bingo and is correct is the winner. The second person is—too late!**

PLAY THE GAME: Scramble the 24 calling cards face down, then select one at random and ask any question about the illustration which elicits the response on that card.

After giving the students enough time to find the correct answer on their Bingo grids, set the card aside and select another card at random and ask a question.

Continue selecting, asking, and setting aside the calling cards until someone says "Bingo!" If no one says *Bingo*, but you notice that someone has five marked squares in a row, point this out and coach them to say *Bingo*!

One student's grid may look like this:

brother-in-law	relatives	grand-daughter	daughter-in-law	niece
parents	uncle	cousin	sister	father-in-law
children	mother-in-law	**FREE**	grand-parents	grandson
nephew	husband	grand-children	brother	sister-in-law
grand-father	aunt	son-in-law	wife	grand-mother

CHECK FOR CORRECT RESPONSES: Have the potential winner read the five winning squares to you.

Check them against the calling cards you have called and set aside. If all five squares are correct, give the winner a prize. Have everyone clear their grids of markers and begin again. "New game!"

If the five squares do not match the items you have called, announce that there is "No Bingo!—Let's continue!"

> **Note:** Do not reveal *which* of their answers is not correct because then other students will begin rearranging their markers according to this information and at least one person, but probably several, will come up a winner without having known the answers on their own, defeating the whole purpose of the exercise.
>
> So make a point of listening to all five of the potential winner's answers before declaring that there is "No Bingo!" And when the students ask, "Which one is wrong?" say that you can't tell them that.

SECTION TWO
GRAMMAR BINGO

INTRODUCTION

These four chapters deal with discrete points of grammar. The first chapter of this section presents a simple TPR lesson for **prepositional phrases** which also reinforces the names of objects, introduces and/or reviews **present and past forms of the verb** *to be* and **adjective-noun word order**, and can even mix in **phonological problems**. The second chapter deals with spelling problems and other generally confusing aspects of **subject pronouns**, and *to be* **contractions** contrasted with **possessive adjectives**. The third chapter includes lessons to teach students to avoid using **double negatives**. It contrasts **negative pronouns** (none, no one, nothing, nowhere, never, neither) with each other as well as with **indefinite pronouns** (any, anyone, anything, anywhere, ever, any time, either) and **inclusive pronouns** (all, everyone, everything, everywhere, always, all the time, both.) The fourth chapter drills **auxiliary verbs**, first addressing **short answers**, from the simplest to the most complex (contrasting all the English auxiliaries including the **modals**,) and then the use of **compound sentences** with **and/but, too/either,** and **so/neither.**

CHAPTER 8

PREPOSITIONAL PHRASES

FOR BEGINNERS AND ESL LITERACY STUDENTS

Here is a game which reinforces lexical items (nouns—the names of any objects you are currently using in your lessons, and the prepositions *in, on, under, between, behind*) while at the same time combining them into prepositional phrases *and* practicing questions with *what* and *where*. It can be done in a 3x3 format, 4x4 or even 5x5, depending on the capabilities of your students and the number of objects you use.

For this example the objects are the props for *Time to Clean House* on page 53 of *Live Action English (Romijn & Seely, Berkeley: Command Performance Language Institute, 1997)*: an *apron*, a can of *kitchen cleanser*, a *sponge*, a *broom*, a *bucket*, a bottle of *liquid* bathroom or kitchen *cleaner*, a *mop*, a *dust cloth*, a *wastebasket*, a small *vacuum cleaner*, and a small *rug*. This lesson is to be done only after the students are familiar and comfortable with the names of the objects.

SET-UP: As the students watch, arrange the objects on a table in front of the class where everyone can easily see most of them. Or have volunteers come to the front and follow your directions to place the objects *in, on, under, between, behind, in front of,* or *next to* each other. For example:

Put the liquid cleaner *in* the bucket. (They'll have to remember this because the bottle probably won't be visible from inside the bucket.)

Put the apron *on* the bucket.

Put the sponge *under* the bucket.   (peeking out a bit so as to be visible)

Put the vacuum cleaner *behind* the bucket.

Put the broom *in front of* the bucket.

Put the kitchen cleanser *in* the wastebasket.

Put the dust cloth *on* the wastebasket.

Put the rug *under* the wastebasket.

Put the mop *between* the bucket and the wastebasket.

Then ask these questions repeatedly until everyone can answer them easily:

1. What's **in** the bucket?	the liquid cleaner
2. What's **on** the bucket?	the apron
3. What's **under** the bucket?	the sponge.
4. What's **behind** the bucket?	the vacuum cleaner
5. What's **in front of** the bucket?	the broom
6. What's **in** the wastebasket?	the kitchen cleanser
7. What's **on** the wastebasket?	the dust cloth
8. What's **under** the wastebasket?	the rug
9. What's **between** the bucket and the wastebasket?	the mop

If you're going to play Bingo with 3x3 Bingo grids (9 squares), limit yourself to these nine questions. If you're going for the 4x4 Bingo format (16 squares), add these seven questions:

10. Where's the wastebasket?	next to the bucket
11. Where's the mop?	between the bucket and the rug
12. Where's the liquid cleaner?	in the bucket
13. Where's the apron?	on the bucket
14. Where's the sponge?	under the bucket
15. Where's the vacuum cleaner?	behind the bucket
16. Where's the broom?	in front of the bucket

Once the students are answering the questions with facility, ask each question one more time, and this time as the whole class answers, *write* the answers on the board.

Or make a written exercise of it by writing the *questions* on the board, having the students copy and answer them on their papers, and then having volunteers come to the board to answer each item so that you can correct them together as the students correct their own papers.

An even better written exercise would be a *dictation* of the questions and answers, followed by volunteers writing it on the board for you to correct.

However you do it, you wind up with the nine or sixteen answers on the board. If you opt for the second or third method of getting them up there, the *questions* will be on the board, too. In this case, after you have made all necessary corrections and *the students have had time to correct their papers*, either erase the questions, leaving the answers alone on the board, or *circle* each answer.

PREPARATION: Give each student a Bingo grid (3x3 or 4x4). Point out that the number of answers on the board is the same as the number of squares on the grid. Tell them to copy one answer into each square. It's important not to copy them in order, so that each person will have a *different* order.

One student's 4x4 grid may look like this:

the mop	in the bucket	the apron	between the bucket and the rug
next to the bucket	the liquid cleaner	the kitchen cleanser	the sponge
the broom	behind the bucket	on the bucket	the dust cloth
the rug	the vacuum cleaner	in front of the bucket	under the bucket

As the students prepare their grids, you can prepare your calling cards (write each answer on one of the blank cards provided or cut up index cards) and hand out bingo markers to each student.

EXPLAIN THE GAME: (Suggested script:) **I'm going to ask one of the questions again. Don't say anything! Just put a marker on the correct answer on your paper. When you have 3 (or 4) squares in a row with markers, say, "Bingo!" They can be horizontal, like this, or vertical, like this, or diagonal, like this. The first person to say *Bingo* and is correct is the winner. The second person is——too late!**

Repeat any of this that is not clear. Try as many examples as necessary to check everyone's comprehension of the procedures and to drill the questions and answers a few more times.

PLAY THE GAME: Scramble the 9 (or 16) calling cards face down, then select one at random and read the corresponding question. After giving the students enough time to find the correct answer on their Bingo grids, set the calling card aside and select another one.

Note: For these games, do *not* continue selecting calling cards *completely* at random. It's a good idea to avoid calling two items of a contrasting pair or set, if possible. If, for example, *"What's in the bucket?"* has already been drawn, then if *"What's on the bucket?"* comes up, set it aside *without* calling it until one of each contrasting set has been drawn. If no one achieves Bingo after one of each set has been called, *then* go back and call the others until someone says Bingo. Why? Whenever two items of a contrasting set are called, if the students confuse the two items, they could get Bingo without having responded to either item correctly. This, of course, defeats the whole purpose of the game.

Continue selecting, asking, and setting aside the calling cards until someone says "Bingo!" If no one says *Bingo*, but you notice that someone has three (or four) marked squares in a row, point this out and coach them to say *Bingo!*

CHECK FOR CORRECT RESPONSES: Have the potential winner read the three (or four) winning squares to you. Check them against the cards you have set aside. If all three or four are correct, give the winner a prize. Have everyone clear their grids of markers and begin again. "New game!"

If the squares do *not* all match the items you have called, announce that there is "No Bingo!—Let's continue!"

Note: Do not reveal *which* of their answers is not correct because then other students will begin rearranging their markers according to this information, and at least one person, but probably several, will come up with a winning combination without having identified the correct endings legitimately.

So make a point of listening to all three (or four) of the potential winner's answers *before* declaring that there is "No Bingo!" And when the students ask, "Which one is not correct?" say that you can't tell them that.

VARIATIONS

On the following pages are several variations which can be used instead of, or in addition to, the foregoing game. Sample sentences are given for each variation.

ADD THE PAST TENSE OF THE VERB *TO BE*: When the students are answering the questions with ease, *rearrange* the objects before them. Then discuss the new arrangement as in the exercise on page 60, this time asking questions about where things *were before* as well as where they are now. The questions might now look like this:

1.	What's **in** the bucket?	the mop
2.	What **was in** the bucket?	the liquid cleaner
3.	What's **on** the bucket?	the rug
4.	What **was on** the bucket?	the apron
5.	What's **under** the bucket?	the dust cloth
6.	What **was under** the bucket?	the sponge
7.	What's **behind** the bucket?	the waste basket
8.	What **was behind** the bucket?	the vacuum cleaner
9.	Where's the liquid cleaner?	behind the wastebasket
10.	Where **was** the liquid cleaner?	in the bucket
11.	Where's the apron?	under the wastebasket
12.	Where **was** the apron?	on the bucket
13.	Where's the sponge?	on the waste basket
14.	Where **was** the sponge?	under the bucket
15.	Where's the vacuum cleaner?	in the waste basket
16.	Where **was** the vacuum cleaner?	behind the bucket

MIX IN PLURAL NOUNS AND FORMS OF THE VERB TO BE: Use objects such as *grapes, beans, gloves, pants, glasses, keys,* in order to add in plural forms of the verb *to be*:

1. What's in the book?	the glasses **are**
2. What **was** in the book?	the keys **were**
3. What's in the hat?	the keys **are**
4. What **was** in the hat?	the glasses **were**
5. What's under the book?	the dictionary **is**
6. What **was** under the book?	the calendar **was**
7. What's on the book?	the calendar **is**
8. What **was** on the book?	the dictionary **was**
etc.	

USE ADJECTIVES: To familiarize students with the English adjective-noun word order, have several similar objects that differ only in size, color, or other single characteristics:

1. What's under the **blue book**?	the **long pencil**
2. What's under the **black book**?	the **short pencil**
3. Where's the **dirty eraser**?	on the **new notebook**
4. Where's the **clean eraser**?	on the **old notebook**
5. What's in the **blue jacket**?	the **neat notebook**
6. What's in the **black jacket**?	the **messy notebook**
7. Where's the **old newspaper**?	under the **long exercise**
8. Where's the **new newspaper**?	under the **short exercise**
etc.	

USE POSSESSIVE -'S WITH STUDENTS' NAMES: Use only objects that belong to the students, to familiarize them with the *-'s* formation of possessive proper nouns as well as the adjective-noun word order:

1. Where are **Raul's** glasses?	in **Tutu's** dictionary
2. Where is **Lucinda's** watch?	under **Mikael's** wallet
3. Where are **Mamie's** glasses?	on **Lisa's** notebook
4. Where is **Maurice's** watch?	on **Si's** notebook
etc.	

INTRODUCE SOME PHONOLOGICAL PROBLEMS: Use objects whose names present your students with troublesome phoneme distinctions, as in **SECTION 3** of this book:

1. Where's the ball?
2. Where's the bowl?
3. Where's the bottle?
4. Where's the butter?
5. Where's the button?
6. Where's the bottom   (of the paper)?
7. Where's the map?
8. Where's the mop?
9. Where's the cat?   (some of these can be toys or figurines)
10. Where's the cot?
11. Where's the cut?   (if pictures are used, prepositions can be *above/below*)
12. Where's the cap?
13. Where's the cop?
14. Where's the cup?
    etc.

CHAPTER 9
PERSONAL PRONOUNS AND POSSESSIVES
FOR BEGINNERS AND ESL LITERACY STUDENTS

This is as much a spelling drill as a grammatical exercise. Some of these contrasts are homonyms—*they're/their, you're/your*; some are phonological problems—*he's/his, I/I'm*; some are simply mentioned too seldom in ESL classes for the students to get familiar enough with them—*we/our*; and some just get confusing because all the others are—*she's/her* (a student who cannot distinguish *you're/your* or *he's/his* will typically use *she's* and *her* interchangeably as well: "She's visiting *she's* mother", instead of "*her* mother"). Here's an opportunity for you to help the students get them all straightened out in their minds, once and for all.

SET-UP: This game is intended as a review for students who have already been presented with subject pronouns, possessive adjectives and contractions in their other lessons. They should be reminded of the difference between the present indicative tense (*He comes to class every day.*) and the present continuous (*He's coming to class now.*) Remind them that the former is used when we talk about an action that takes place with some frequency or regularity in the present, and the latter is used when we're talking about an action that is happening as we speak. They also may need a review of the contractions with the verb *to be*:

  I am=I'm, you are =you're, he is=he's, she is=she's, etc.

After reviewing these concepts, give the class the following written exercise as a dictation, or as a cloze (where the underlined words would be blanked out by you, to be filled in by the students):

1. *They* live in New York.
2. I remember *their* father.
3. *They're* playing Bingo.

4. It's nice to meet *you.*
5. Let me see *your* book.
6. *You're* listening to the teacher.

7. *She's* eating lunch.
8. That's *her* house.

9. *He* speaks Spanish.
10. *He's* talking to David.
11. This is *his* brother.

12. *We* speak Japanese.
13. *We're* not dancing.
14. Do you like *our* classroom?

15. *I* don't know.
16. *I'm* crying.

Volunteers then go to the board to write the complete sentences so that you can all correct them together as the students correct their own papers. Practice pronunciation as needed. *Circle the underlined words.*

PREPARATION: Give each student a 4x4 Bingo grid. Point out that there are 16 sentences on the board and 16 squares on their Bingo grids. Tell them to copy one *circled* word into each square. It's important not to copy them in order, so that each person will have a *different* order.

One student's grid may look like this:

I'm	her	they	we
their	you	I	his
you're	they're	he	we're
he's	our	your	she's

As the students prepare their grids, you can hand out markers to each student. The calling cards are provided with this book.

EXPLAIN THE GAME: (Suggested script:) **I'm going to read one of the words on your Bingo paper. Then I'll use it in a sentence so that you will understand which word it is. Remember that in English we usually don't spell words the way they sound, so you have to listen, but more than that, you have to *think, too*, about which word you hear. Don't say anything! Just put a marker on the correct answer on your paper. When you have 4 squares in a row with markers, say, "Bingo!" They can be horizontal, like this, or vertical, like this, or diagonal, like this. The first person to say *Bingo* and is correct is the winner. The second person is—too late!**

Repeat any of this that is not clear. Try as many examples as necessary to check everyone's comprehension of the procedures and to drill the questions and answers a few more times.

PLAY THE GAME: Scramble the 16 calling cards face down, then select one at random and read the word written on it, followed by a sentence using the word. You can stick to the sentences in the exercise for a very simple Bingo game for students who have only a very shaky grasp of the concepts involved. For students who are a little more on top of the material, make up *original* sentences that they will understand. After giving the students enough time to find the correct answer on their Bingo grids, set the calling card aside and select another one.

Note: For these games, do *not* continue selecting calling cards *completely* at random. It's a good idea to avoid calling two items of a contrasting pair or set, if possible. If, for example, *you're* has already been drawn, then if *your* comes up, set it aside *without* calling it until one of each contrasting set has been drawn. If no one achieves Bingo after one of each set has been called, *then* go back and call the others until someone says Bingo. Why? Whenever two items of a contrasting set are called, if the students confuse the two items, they could get Bingo without having responded to either item correctly. This, of course, defeats the whole purpose of the game.

Continue selecting, reading words and using them in sentences, and setting aside the calling cards until someone says "Bingo!" If no one says *Bingo*, but you notice that someone has four marked squares in a row, point this out and coach them to say *Bingo*!

CHECK FOR CORRECT RESPONSES: Have the potential winner read the four winning squares to you. Check them against the cards you have set aside. If all four are correct, give the winner a prize. Have everyone clear their grids of markers and begin again. "New game!"

If the squares do *not* all match the items you have called, announce that there is "No Bingo!—Let's continue!"

Note: Do not reveal *which* of their answers is not correct because then other students will begin rearranging their markers according to this information, and at least one person, but probably several, will come up with a winning combination without having identified the correct endings legitimately.

So make a point of listening to all four of the potential winner's answers *before* declaring that there is "No Bingo!" And when the students ask, "Which one is not correct?" say that you can't tell them that.

5X5 VARIATION: ADD OBJECT PRONOUNS for High Beginners

Copy onto the board something similar to the following table (or use an overhead projector):

PERSON	SUBJECT	CONTRACTION	POSSESSIVE	OBJECT
1st singular	I	I am = **I'm**	**my**	**me**
1st plural	**we**	we are = **we're**	**our**	**us**
2nd sing. & plural	**you**	you are = **you're**	**your**	you
3rd sing. feminine	**she**	she is = **she's**	**her**	her
3rd sing. masculine	**he**	he is = **he's**	**his**	**him**
3rd sing.—no gender	**it**	it is = **it's**	its	it
3rd plural	**they**	they are = **they're**	**their**	**them**

Begin with just the first person singular. Explain the difference between *I, I'm, my,* and *me*. Give examples of sentences for each:

> *I* study English every day.
> *I'm* studying English right now.
> That is *my* book.
> Please give it to *me*.

Practice this some more by giving the students a few more sentences with each word.

Next go thru each additional person in the same way. When the bottom of the chart is reached, add *there* even tho it doesn't fit any of the categories at hand. There are two reasons for this: a) *there* is another homonym typically confused with *they're* and *their*, and b) 25 different words are needed for the 5x5 Bingo grid. (It is suggested that *its* be left out at this time. The difference between *it's* and *its* is a fine point that most *native* speakers don't seem to have mastered, perhaps because the written form of *its* is not a word in frequent enough use. Whatever the reason, it's probably not a productive use of the students' time at this early stage of their acquisition of English. But *add it* if you don't agree!)

Now practice the entire chart, mixing sentences using *each* word printed in bold type. As in the previous game, begin by pronouncing one of the words and then use it in a sentence that the students will understand. The words which show up in two places on the chart (*you, her, it*) should be used in sentences for *either* usage.

Finally, have the students fill in their Bingo grids (circle the words in bold type for them to copy into the 25 squares) and explain and play the game as on pages 67 and 68, but now with 5x5 Bingo grids.

As a follow-up exercise, give the students a dictation of some of the sentences used for the game.

CHAPTER 10
INDEFINITE PRONOUNS
FOR HIGH BEGINNERS AND LOW INTERMEDIATE STUDENTS

LESSONS: Here is a series of short lessons to prepare students for the Bingo game at the end of this chapter. Each takes about thirty minutes.

Introduce the negative words: Ask the students questions which will elicit different negative answers, providing them with the correct word:

1. Look, everybody, *who's* behind (Carlos)?   **Nobody** or **No one**.
    (Substitute the name of a student sitting in the *back* of the room.)

(At this time, limit yourself to one or the other, **nobody** or **no one,** depending on the level and experience of your students. Students with a lot of aural experience are probably already familiar with the word *nobody* but not with *no one*. If this lesson is going to be a big challenge for them, you may want to stick with the more familiar and not bother them with the unfamiliar form *no one*. If they *need* a good stretch, however, introduce the term *no one* and tell them that it means exactly the same as *nobody*.)

2. *What's* behind him?   **Nothing.**
    (Referring to someone with *nothing* on the wall behind him.)

(Point out the difference between the first question with *who*, which is a question about *people*, and the second question with *what*, which is a question about *things*. Then the answers will be *nobody* or *no one*, which mean *no person*; or *nothing*, which means *no thing*.)

3. (Ask a young person) How many grandchildren do you have?   **None.**

(Point out that *none* means *zero*. It's the number *zero*, and it can refer to people *or* things. We use it to answer questions with *how many?* or *how much?*)

4. Are you going home now? No.   Where are you going?   **Nowhere.**

5. Are you planning to go to the moon? No. When are you going to the moon?   **Never.**

6. How often do you go to school? Every day. How often do you go swimming?   **Never.**

(Point out that when the question is *where,* about *places*, the negative answer is *nowhere*. When the question is *when* or *how often*, about time or frequency, the negative answer is *never*.)

7. Which pencil is black, this one or this one?   **Neither one.**

(When the question is *which one*, where you have a choice of two, the negative answer is *neither one*.)

As you introduce each of the six negative words, write it on the board:

no one   nowhere   none   nothing   never   neither one

Written exercise: You may want to ask a few more questions orally for additional practice before trying the written exercise on the following page (which you have permission to duplicate for ESL classroom use):

NEGATIVES (Lesson 1)

| nobody | nowhere | none | nothing | never | neither one |

Choose one of these negative words to answer each question.

Negative answers only!   Short answers only (one word only)!

1. Who are you talking to? _____

2. What do you have under your chair? _____

3. Which woman are you going to marry, Sally or Sue? _____

4. How much money do you have? _____

5. Where did you go last night? _____

6. How often do you go swimming? _____

7. How many dogs do you have? _____

8. Who do you see behind Margarita? _____

9. Which dress do you like, the green one or the purple one? _____

10. When are you going to get married? _____

11. What are you doing? _____

12. Where are you going? _____

Correcting the papers: After the students have written in their selections for each question, go over them orally together. As they give you the correct short answer for each question, repeat that short answer, and then, in order to expose them to the long answers (providing *comprehensible input*), quickly state the long response as well. For example, for number one—*Who are you talking to?*—the students will say, *No one!* Your response: *That's right; No one—I'm not talking to anyone!*

More whole group practice: Next, ask them the same questions again, in random order, not allowing them to consult their papers for the correct short answer.

Pair practice: When they seem to be able to provide the short answers with ease, have them ask each other the questions in pairs. Emphasize that only *one person* should be looking at the paper to read the questions. The other person should *listen*, not look at the paper, and answer with short answers.

Introducing the long answers: Now explain that these negative words are *not* used in *complete sentences* because in English we don't like to use *double negatives*, that is, two negative words in one phrase. Therefore, if you answer the second question—*What do you have under your chair?*—with a complete sentence, the answer would be *I don't have* **anything** *under my chair.* It's not correct to say *I don't have* **nothing** *under my chair,* because the words *don't (do* **not***)* and **nothing** are both negative, making a double negative and we don't like double negatives in English.

Go thru the other questions in the exercise and provide the long answers for each one, trying not to give the students enough time to copy it all down in writing, but just to keep them focused on the sound and comprehension of the sentences. Write the indefinite pronoun to be used in place of each negative near the appropriate negative word on the board:

no one	nowhere	none	nothing	never	neither one
anyone	anywhere	any	anything	ever	either one

Written exercise: Have the students go back to the written exercise and try to write the long answer to each question in the spaces provided. Remind them to pay attention to the *verb tense* of each question.

Correcting the papers: After the students have completed the exercise, have volunteers write the sentences on the board so that you can go over them and correct them together while the students correct their own papers. Point out that the word order for items 6 and 10, containing *never/ever*, is a little different from the word order of the other items. Instead of "I don't go swimming *ever,*" we usually say, "I don't *ever* go swimming."

Practice pronunciation: Go over the pronunciation of each question, answer, and any difficult individual words.

Pair practice: Have them repeat the pair practice, this time responding with long answers instead of short. Again, emphasize that only *one person* should be looking at the paper to read the questions. The other person should *listen*, not look at the paper, and answer with long answers.

NEXT DAY'S LESSON: In the following class session, review the entire lesson using the written exercise on the page 76.

THIRD LESSON: After the foregoing lessons, some students will tend to *overuse* the indefinite forms, automatically substituting them in *all* cases where they previously would have used the negative forms, even for the short answers. For example, you might hear a student answer the question *Who are you talking to?* with the short answer *Anyone!* when they really mean *No one!* For this reason, this third exercise was developed to *contrast* the two sets of words—the negatives and the indefinites. It can be presented either immediately following the second day's lesson (during the same class session) *or* on the following day.

Begin by explaining that the words *nothing* and *anything* do not have the same meaning. One is neutral and the other is negative. *Anything* is similar in meaning to *nothing* only in a sentence where it is combined with the negative word *not*. (Refer to examples from the two written exercises for *anything/nothing* and similarly for the other pairs as well.)

Next, distribute copies of the written exercise on page 77, "Long and Short Answers". Go thru it together, explaining what is meant by the affirmative, indefinite responses (*I don't care where I go—I just want to go away!*), eliciting the negative answers from the students. Point out that you can give either a short or a long reply whether your answer is negative or affirmative. Here the students can plainly see that the short answer *Anywhere!* to the first question is the *opposite* of the short answer *Nowhere!*

Note that again the *time* sentence (number 6) is a little different from the others, using a different indefinite *Any time!* from the one (*ever*) used in the previous exercises.

Written exercise: Give the students a few more minutes to complete the negative answers if they have not already done so.

Pair practice: Have the students ask each other questions and practice answering both with negative and affirmative, long and short responses.

Permission granted to duplicate the following two pages for ESL classroom use.

NEGATIVES (Lesson 2)

nobody	nowhere	none	nothing	never	neither one

Choose one of these negative words to answer each question.

Negative answers only!   Short answers only (one word only)!

1. What do you have in your hand? _____

2. Who are you looking for? _____

3. Where did you go yesterday?   _____

4. How many grandchildren do you have?   _____

5. Which hat do you like, the big one or the little one?   _____

6. How often do you get sick? _____

7. How much beer did you drink? _____

8. Who do you know in Washington, D.C.?   _____

9. Which ice cream do you want, the chocolate or the vanilla? _____

10. When are you going to go to the doctor? _____

11. Where are you going to go for your vacation? _____

12. What did you say? _____

Puppies Or Poppies? ESL Bingo ©1998 Elizabeth Kuizenga Romijn, Command Performance (510) 524-1191

LONG AND SHORT ANSWERS (Lesson 3)

What are the negative answers for each question, both long and short?

1. Where do you want to go for a vacation?   **Negative answers:**

    Short answers: Anywhere!   *Nowhere!*

    Long answers: I want to go anywhere!   *I don't want to go anywhere!*

2. Who do you want to talk to about your problems?

    Short answers: Anybody!   _____

    Long answers: I want to talk to anybody! _____

3. What do you want for your birthday?

    Short answers: Anything!   _____

    Long answers: I want anything! _____

4. How much money do you want to win?

    Short answers: Any amount! _____

    Long answers: I want to win any amount of money! _____

5. Who do you want to see, your father or your mother?

    Short answers: Either one! _____

    Long answers: I want to see either one! _____

6. When can I visit you again?

    Short answers: Any time! _____

    Long answers: You can visit me any time! _____

Puppies Or Poppies? ESL Bingo ©1998 Elizabeth Kuizenga Romijn, Command Performance (510) 524-1191

Inclusives: Finally, add the inclusive pronouns to the paradigm on the board:

no one	nowhere	none (of them)	nothing	never	neither one
anyone	anywhere	any (of them)	anything	ever	either one
everyone	everywhere	all (of them)	everything	always	both (of them)
				every time	

Pose the following questions orally, asking the whole class to select one of the inclusive pronouns to answer each question:

1. How often do we speak English in this class?   (always, all the time)
2. Which one of these pencils is yellow?   (both of them)
3. Who do you like in this class?   (everyone)
4. What do you like about this school?   (everything)
5. Where in the world can you find insects?   (everywhere)
6. How many of your children do you love?   (all of them)

Repeat the same questions in a written exercise. Either dictate the questions, or write them on the board for the students to copy, or distribute the questions on paper. Have them write both short and long answers. Follow with pronunciation and pair practice, students asking each other and answering the same questions.

BINGO

SET-UP: Write the following six questions on the board. Then ask the class for a short negative answer to each one. Once the negative answers are written on the board, ask for a *long* negative answer to each one, writing these on the board as the students provide them. Finally, ask for an *inclusive* answer to each one, also writing these answers under the questions as you elicit them.

What do you like about this school?		**Nothing.**
	I don't like	**anything.**
	I like	**everything.**
Who are you going to invite to your party?		**No one.**
	I'm not going to invite	**anyone.**
	I'm going to invite	**everyone.**
Where does she like to drive?		**Nowhere.**
	She doesn't like to drive	**anywhere.**
	She likes to drive	**everywhere.**
Which shirt do you like, the striped one or the plaid one?		**Neither one.**
	I don't like	**either one.**
	I like	**both of them.**
How many of your children will you bring to school?		**None of them.**
	I won't bring	**any of them.**
	I'll bring	**all of them.**
How much of this coffee are you going to drink?		**None of it.**
	I'm not going to drink	**any of it.**
	I'm going to drink	**all of it.**

PREPARATION: On the board, circle the 18 words or phrases printed on page 79 in bold type. Give each student a 4x4 Bingo grid. Point out that there are 16 squares on their Bingo grids and 18 answers on the chalkboard. Point to one of the answers and tell them to copy it into one of the squares. After allowing enough time for everyone to do this, point to a second answer and tell them to copy it into another square. Tell them that for Bingo everyone needs to have a different order, so urge them not to copy them all in the order they see on the board. Also point out that each person will have to leave two answers out.

One student's grid may look like this, where *everybody* and *none of them* have been left out:

everywhere	any of it	nothing	all of it
anything	nobody	either one	any of them
neither one	everything	nowhere	both of them
anybody	anywhere	all of them	none of it

While the students are preparing their grids, give each student a handful of markers. The calling cards for this game are provided with this book.

EXPLAIN THE GAME: (Suggested script:) **I'm going to ask one of the questions on the board. If I shake my head like this, find the correct short negative answer on your paper and put a marker on it. If I tell you the beginning of the answer, for example, "She doesn't like to drive ____" [shake your head], or "She likes to drive ____" [nod your head], find the correct ending on your paper and put a marker on it. When you have 4 squares in a row with markers, say "Bingo!" They can be horizontal, like this, or vertical, like this, or diagonal, like this. The first person to say *Bingo* and is correct is the winner. The second person is——too late!**

Repeat any of this that is not clear. Try as many examples as necessary to check everyone's comprehension of the procedures.

PLAY THE GAME: Scramble the 18 calling cards face down, then select one at random and ask the question from the board which will elicit the answer you have drawn.

After giving the students enough time to find the correct answer on their Bingo grids, set the calling card aside and select another one.

Note: For these games, do *not* continue selecting calling cards *completely* at random. It's a good idea to avoid calling two items of a contrasting pair or set, if possible. If, for example, *nowhere* has already been drawn, then if *anywhere* or *everywhere* comes up, set it aside *without* calling it until one of each contrasting set has been drawn. If no one achieves Bingo after one of each set has been called, *then* go back and call the others until someone says *Bingo*. Why? Whenever two items of a contrasting set are called, if the students confuse the two items, they could get Bingo without having responded to either item correctly. This, of course, defeats the whole purpose of the game.

Continue selecting, asking, and setting aside the calling cards until someone says "Bingo!" If no one says *Bingo*, but you notice that someone has four marked squares in a row, point this out and coach them to say *Bingo*!

CHECK FOR CORRECT RESPONSES: Have the potential winner read the four winning squares to you.

Check them against the cards you have called and set aside. If all four squares are correct, give the winner a prize. Have everyone clear their grids of markers and begin again. "New game!"

If the four squares do not all match the items you have called, announce that there is "No Bingo!—Let's continue!"

Note: Do not reveal *which* of their answers is not correct because then other students will begin rearranging their markers according to this information and at least one person, but probably several, will come up with a winning combination without having identified the correct responses legitimately.

So make a point of listening to all four of the potential winner's answers *before* declaring that there is "No Bingo!" And when the students ask, "Which one is not correct?" say that you can't tell them that.

SUGGESTED FOLLOW-UP LESSONS AND BINGO GAMES

After the introduction of this material, more practice may be created by adapting these lessons to other contexts you are discussing in your lessons. For example, many of the lessons in *Live Action English (Romijn & Seely, Berkeley: Command Performance Language Institute, 1997)* provide excellent contexts for more practice contrasting some of the pronouns presented in this chapter.

Consider *Going to the Movies* on page 39 of *Live Action English*:

1.   Go to the movie theater.

2.   Buy a ticket.

3.   Give it to the ticket-taker at the door.

4.   Go into the lobby.

5.   Buy some popcorn and something to drink.

6.   Go into the theater.

7.   Look for a good seat. Here's one. Sit down.

8.   Watch the movie and smile.

9.   Oh, this part is sad. Cry.

10.   Wipe your eyes.

11.   This part is scary. Open your eyes wide and scream.

12.   This part is funny. Laugh.

13.   Now the movie is over. Clap.

14.   Get up and leave.

15.   How did you like it?

Once the students are familiar with the vocabulary in this lesson, you can refer to one of the students who performed the series during the presentation of the lesson, asking these past tense questions:

1. When did she go to the movie theater?   **Yesterday.**

2. When did she go to the *police*?   **Never.**

3. How many tickets did she buy?   **One.**

4. How many *movies* did she buy?   **None.**

5.   *or:*   She didn't buy   **any.**

6. Who did she give her ticket to?   **The ticket-taker.**

7. Who did she give her *popcorn* to?   **Nobody.**

8.   *or:*   She didn't give it to   **anybody.**

9. Where did she go after she bought her popcorn?   **Into the theater.**

10. Where did she go *during* the movie?   **Nowhere.**

11.   *or:*   She didn't go   **anywhere.**

12. What did she look for in the theater?   **A good seat.**

13. What did she look for in the *lobby*?   **Nothing.**

14.   *or:*   She didn't look for   **anything.**

15. Who did she go with, Jaime or Chin?   **Neither one.**

16.   *or:*   She didn't go with   **either one.**

This can be used first as an oral exercise, then as a written dictation, then as pair practice, and finally as a Bingo game, as on pages 79-81.

CHAPTER 11
AUXILIARY VERBS

The English system of auxiliary verbs is perhaps the most difficult aspect of English grammar for speakers of other languages to learn, partly because of its complexity, but also because of the fact that it is so foreign—few languages have anything like it, especially the way auxiliaries are used *alone* in English phrases.

Because of this difficulty, and because the auxiliary verb system is so fundamental to understanding the English use of verbs and verb tenses, it is useful to familiarize students at the lowest levels of English acquisition with its use in normal conversation. One simple way we use it overtly is in short answers—simple if you limit yourself to one or two auxiliaries at a time. Students often get all the way to advanced stages of fluency without ever understanding even this elementary use of auxiliaries, answering yes/no questions with a large variety of auxiliaries but never selecting the correct one! (Did you see him? Yes, it is. Will they recognize you? No, they don't.)

However, if students are guided thru the correct selection of person, tense and auxiliary verbs from the most rudimentary levels of their acquisition of English, they come out with a basic understanding of the way the system works, and they have no problem sorting thru all the choices available to them later at the more advanced levels.

What is so fundamentally important about the English auxiliary system and what is the value of spending so much time and effort to help students grasp it? English auxiliaries mark person, tense, voice, and modality—concepts which in other languages are marked in entirely different ways, such as with hundreds of verb forms. In English, what our paltry four or five forms of each verb lack in number, our auxiliary system makes up for in intricacy. Until ESL students understand this basic difference between our verb system and their own, many things we do with verbs in English elude them as subtlety or outright mystery.

This chapter includes 10 Bingo games which drill students on the correct selection of auxiliaries for **short answers**, beginning with the simplest, and working up to the use of *all* the English auxiliaries which are used for short answers. An eleventh game practices **compound sentences** *with **and**, **but**, **too** and **either***, and the twelfth and final game practices responses with *so* and ***neither***.

SHORT ANSWERS
For Beginning, Intermediate and ESL Literacy Students

GAME 1: VERB *TO Be* for Beginners and Literacy Students

LESSON: Orally, ask the whole class and also ask individual students questions similar to the ones in the following exercise.

SHORT ANSWERS—Verb to Be

1. Is (Peter) here today? _____*Yes, he is.*_____
   [Substitute the name of a male student who is present today.]

2. Is (Sandra) here? _____*No, she isn't.*_____
   [Substitute the name of a female student who is absent today.]

3. Are (Ben and Nicasio) brothers? _____*No, they aren't.*_____
   [Substitute the names of two students who are not brothers.]

4. Are we in (San Francisco)? _____*Yes, we are.*_____
   [Substitute the name of the city you are in.]

5. Is today (Friday)? _____*Yes, it is.*_____
   [Substitute the current day of the week.]

6. Are (Sasha and Olga) from (Russia)? _____*Yes, they are.*_____
   [Substitute the names of two students and their country.]

7. Is (Brenda) here? _____*Yes, she is.*_____
   [Substitute the name of a female student who is present today.]

8. Is it (9:17 a.m.)? _____*No, it isn't*_____

9. Is (Noel) here today? _____*No, he isn't*_____
   [Substitute the name of a male student who is absent today.]

10. Are we (watching TV)? _____*No, we aren't.*_____

11. Am I a student in this class? _____ *No, you aren't.*

12. Are you hungry? _____ *No, I'm not.*

When students answer with a simple **yes** or **no**, coach them and encourage them to answer with the correct short answer. If you have never shown them a paradigm of the verb **to be,** put one on the board or overhead projector for them now:

I am
she is
he is
it is

we are
you are
they are

After *orally* asking and answering questions like these over the course of a week or so (several class sessions), *write* similar questions on the board. Have them copy them and write the correct short answers.

If your class has literacy problems, list the possible short answers for your written exercise so that the students need only *match and/or copy* the correct answers to the questions. Go thru several of the items together, pointing out that the person in the answer must be the same as the person in the question.

Note: You may of course prepare a similar exercise on *paper* and give each student a copy of it to complete. However, there are two major reasons to use the chalkboard or overhead instead. First, it allows you to point out, circle and otherwise emphasize the connection between the question and the answer. Second, it allows you to tailor the questions to the students who are actually present in your class, as well as to the circumstances, such as weather conditions (Is it raining right now? Is it cold in here?) at the time of the exercise. The added bonus is that you have that much less preparation and paper to carry around before class.

When everyone knows the correct short answer for each question, have them practice in pairs, one student reading the questions and the other student answering *without reading the paper or the chalkboard.* When they are finished, have them change roles so that the first student is now answering, instead of asking, the questions, and vice versa.

Another useful extension of this exercise is to give the students a *dictation* of similar (or exactly the same) questions and short answers, especially if your students are better at oral production than they are at written.

SET-UP: One more time, orally ask the students 10 questions similar to the questions on the previous two pages. As they answer, write the short answers on the board:

Yes, it is.   Yes, she is.   Yes, he is.
No, it isn't.   No, she isn't.   No, he isn't.

Yes, we are.   Yes, they are.
No, we aren't.   No, they aren't.

Leave out the first person singular and the second person for now. It can be unnecessarily confusing for the students to have to decide between *Yes, you are* and *Yes, I am* for questions such as *Are you a student?* (It is fairly obvious in natural conversation to come up with the appropriate response, but beginning language students can easily become confused by this when they have enough time for a written exercise or a Bingo response.)

PREPARATION: Give each student a 3x3 Bingo grid. Point out that there are 9 squares on their Bingo grids and 10 answers on the chalkboard. Point to one of the answers and tell them to copy it into one of the squares. After allowing enough time for everyone to do this, point to a second answer and tell them to copy it into another square. Tell them that for Bingo everyone needs to have a different order, so urge them not to copy them all in the order they see on the board. Also point out that each person will have to leave one answer out.

One student's grid may look like this, where *No, she isn't* has been left out:

No, he isn't.	No, they aren't.	Yes, it is.
No, it isn't.	Yes, he is.	Yes, we are.
No, we aren't.	Yes, she is.	Yes, they are.

While the students are preparing their grids, give each student several markers. The calling cards for these games are provided with this book.

EXPLAIN THE GAME: (Suggested script:) **I'm going to ask a question such as "Is Maria here today?" Don't answer! Find the correct answer on your paper and put a marker on it. When you have 3 squares in a row with markers, say "Bingo!" They can be horizontal, like this, or vertical, like this, or diagonal, like this. The first person to say *Bingo* and is correct is the winner. The second person is—too late!**

Repeat any of this that is not clear. Try as many examples as necessary to check everyone's comprehension of the procedures.

PLAY THE GAME: Scramble the 10 calling cards (provided) face down, then select one at random and ask any question *familiar to the students* which will elicit the answer you have drawn.

After giving the students enough time to find the correct answer on their Bingo grids, set the calling card aside and select another one.

Continue selecting, asking, and setting aside the calling cards until someone says "Bingo!" If no one says *Bingo*, but you notice that someone has three marked squares in a row, point this out and coach them to say *Bingo*!

CHECK FOR CORRECT RESPONSES: Have the potential winner read the three winning squares to you.

Check them against the cards you have called and set aside. If all three squares are correct, give the winner a prize. Have everyone clear their grids of markers and begin again. "New game!"

If the three squares do not all match the items you have called, announce that there is "No Bingo!—Let's continue!"

Note: Do not reveal *which* of their answers is not correct because then other students will begin rearranging their markers according to this information and at least one person, but probably several, will come up with a winning combination without having identified the correct responses legitimately.

So make a point of listening to all three of the potential winner's answers *before* declaring that there is "No Bingo!" And when the students ask, "Which one is not correct?" say that you can't tell them that.

GAME 2: 4x4 VARIATION WITH *DO* for Beginners and Literacy Students

As students progress and begin to use the verb *to do*, play Short Answer Bingo in which short answers with *do* have been mixed in, as in the following exercise. (You may find it necessary to play Bingo with *only* the verb **to do** before trying to mix them.)

Is it raining?	**Do** you like the rain?
Is (Vladmir) married?	**Does** he have any grandchildren?
Are you married?	**Do** you have any grandchildren?
Is (Ana) from (Venezuela)?	**Does** she live in (Venezuela) now?
Are we playing Bingo?	**Do** we play Bingo every Friday?

Use 4x4 grids instead of 3x3s. Leaving out *first person singular* and *second person*, as in the simpler version above, you now have 20 short answers for 16 squares on the Bingo grids:

Yes, he is.	No, he isn't.	Yes, he does.	No, he doesn't.
Yes, she is.	No, she isn't.	Yes, she does.	No, she doesn't.
Yes, it is.	No, it isn't.	Yes, it does.	No, it doesn't.
Yes, we are.	No, we aren't.	Yes, we do.	No, we don't.
Yes, they are.	No, they aren't.	Yes, they do.	No, they don't.

One student's grid may look like this (with or without the words *yes* and *no*—see GAME 4 for the reason for the parentheses here):

(Yes,) it does.	(No,) she doesn't.	(Yes,) they do.	(No,) we don't.
(No,) he isn't.	(No,) they don't.	(Yes,) she is.	(No,) it isn't.
(Yes,) she does.	(Yes,) we are.	(No,) it doesn't.	(No,) they aren't.
(Yes,) they are.	(Yes,) he does.	(Yes,) we do.	(No,) she isn't.

GAME 3: 5x5 VARIATION WITH *DO, THERE IS/THERE ARE*

for Beginners and Literacy Students

This game is similar to Game 2, with the addition of:

Yes, there is.	No, there isn't.
Yes, there are.	No, there aren't.

This brings the total number of short answers to 24, so a 5x5 Bingo grid can be used with the center square marked FREE.

GAME 4: *YES/NO* VARIATION

For Games 1 or 2 above, have the students copy the short answers in their grids *without* the words *yes* and *no*. Then, altho this will not sound as natural as the language in the other games, *you will give them the answer yes or no* following the questions as you call them. For example:

"Is Hilda hungry? Yes, ..."	[Students mark *she is.*]
"Does she have an apple? No, ..."	[Students mark *she doesn't.*]

There are two major reasons for doing it this way:

1. Asking only questions whose answers the students already know, as in the first games above, limits the number and variety of questions that can be used. (Maybe you're the only one who *knows* that Hilda is hungry or that she doesn't have an apple, or something even more interesting than these fun facts!) When *you* are providing the answers *yes* or *no*, the students don't need to know that part of the answer. Their problem then is only to identify the correct pronoun and auxiliary verb for the remainder of the short answer.

2. Many slower students need some time to catch on to the negative forms of the short answers. Separating them from the words *yes* and *no* will guide them to notice these negative endings, to learn the rule that *yes* answers must be followed by *affirmative* short answers and *no* answers must be followed by *negative* short answers, and to discriminate between the two.

GAME 5: *PRESENT/PAST* VARIATION for Beginners and Literacy Students

As students progress and begin to work with the **past tense**, add the past forms of *be* and *do* to their repertoire of short answers, as in the following exercise:

SHORT ANSWERS—Be, Do

1. Are you married? _____

2. Are you single? _____

3. Do you have children? _____

4. Do you have grandchildren? _____

5. Does your sister have children? _____

6. Did you see your sister yesterday? _____

7. Was she in [the city where your class is held] yesterday?

   _____

8. Is she in [the city where your class is held] now?

   _____

9. Were you in class yesterday? _____

10. Was Martha here yesterday? _____

Here is a paradigm you may or may not want to put on the board for your more academically inclined students:

	present **be**	past **be**	present **do**	past **do**
I	am	was	do	did
she he it	is	was	does	did
you we they	are	were	do	did

At this level, they are probably no longer having any problem identifying the correct *pronoun* to use. The big problem remaining is the choice of *auxiliary verb*, so now *that* becomes the only word for the students to copy into their Bingo grids.

But this leaves us with only 14 choices for 16 squares, so let's add the modal *can* which the students are also probably ready to handle at this level:

11. Can you see the moon tonight? _____

12. Can you see the rain? _____

Here are the 16 choices you write on the board for this game as the students answer your questions with short answers:

is	are	was	were
isn't	aren't	wasn't	weren't
do	does	did	can
don't	doesn't	didn't	can't

One student's grid may look like this:

can't	don't	did	wasn't
was	are	is	does
doesn't	were	can	weren't
didn't	isn't	aren't	do

GAME 6: *WILL FUTURE* VARIATION for High Beginners

At this level, as the students are learning to use the **future tense with *will***, play Short Answer Bingo with the auxiliary *will* mixed in with *do* and *be* (and, optionally, *can*).

Will you be here tomorrow?	Yes, I will.
Will I see you on Saturday?	No, you won't.

Here we have 16 (without *can* and *can't*) or 18 (with *can* and *can't*) choices for the Bingo grids:

is, isn't,	was, wasn't,	are, aren't,	were, weren't,
do, don't	does, doesn't	did, didn't	will, won't

(can, can't)

One student's grid might look like this:

weren'T	is	did	wasn'T
was	are	isn'T	does
doesn'T	were	don'T	will
didn'T	won'T	aren'T	do

GAME 7: 5x5 MODAL VARIATION for High Beginning and Intermediate Levels

At this level, as the students are learning and hopefully acquiring the rest of the **Modal Auxiliaries** and the **Conditional** with **would,** mix these auxiliaries into Short Answer Bingo.

In conversational Standard American English, only a few of the modals are used for both questions *and* answers. Eliminated by this requirement of our game are **must, might,** and **shall.** Therefore, for Short Answer Bingo, we won't use such formal and/or unnatural language as:

Must I call?   Yes, you must.

Might they be late?   No, they mightn't.

Shall we dance?   No, we shan't.

Instead, we will confine ourselves to the use of **would, should, could**, and (optionally) **may**:

Would you like to go now?	Yes, I would.
Would you learn English if you still lived in your country?	No, I wouldn't.
Should she see a doctor?	Yes, she should.
Could you understand English two years ago?	No, I couldn't.
May I see the photos?	Yes, you may.

For this variation, then, so far we have 26 choices for 25 squares. At this level we can also add *am* and *am not* without too much confusion, to bring the total to 28:

am   am not   is   isn't   are   aren't

            was   wasn't   were   weren't

do   don't   does   doesn't   did   didn't

will   won't   would   wouldn't   should   shouldn't

can   can't   could   couldn't   (may   may not)

One student's grid might look like this:

am not	don't	did	shouldn't	wasn't
was	are	would	won't	does
doesn't	were	can	isn't	couldn't
will	is	could	am	weren't
should	wouldn't	aren't	can't	do

GAME 8: 4X4 *HAVE/DO/BE* VARIATION for Intermediate Students

At this level, as the students are learning and hopefully acquiring the **present perfect tense**, play Short Answer Bingo with the auxiliary *have* mixed in with *do* and *be* as in the exercise on the next page.

Here we have 18 choices for the Bingo grids:

is, isn't   was, wasn't   are, aren't   were, weren't
do, don't   does, doesn't   did, didn't
have, haven't   has, hasn't

One student's grid might look like this:

hasn't	don't	did	wasn't
was	are	have	does
doesn't	were	can	haven't
didn't	has	aren't	do

SHORT ANSWERS

1. Have you ever been to [name of local park]? _____

2. Did you like it? _____

3. Do you go there often? _____

4. Does your mother always go with you? _____

5. Has she ever gone with you? _____

6. Are [names of two students] eating lunch? _____

7. Have they already eaten lunch today? _____

8. Did they eat in the cafeteria this morning? _____

9. Were they late to class today? _____

10. Are they usually late? _____

11. Were you late today? _____

12. Do you have a lot of things to do? *_____

* Note that the auxiliary verb here is *do*, not *have*. *Have* is the principle verb in this question, so the correct short answer is *Yes, I do*, not *Yes, I have*.

GAME 9: 5X5 *HAVE/DO/BE* VARIATION for High Intermediate

As your students are learning the **past perfect tense**, have them play Short Answer Bingo with the auxiliaries *had* and *hadn't* mixed in with the other auxiliaries in Games 7 or 8, using as many or as few as your students can handle at a time. You may want to cut it down to fewer than 24 choices and use 4x4 grids instead of 5x5s.

GAME 10: 5X5 ALL-AUXILIARY VARIATION

for Intermediate and Advanced Students

Finally, for intermediate and advanced students who are familiar with *all* the English auxiliary verbs but need some remediation to help them learn to select the correct one for a given short answer, play Bingo with all the English auxiliaries mixed together (with the exception of *must*, *might*, and *shall*—see Game 7).

You may be surprised to find that this is too much of a challenge for even advanced students, and that you need to back up to some of the previous games in order to work up to this one over the course of several weeks.

Here is the complete list of the auxiliaries to write on the board as the students answer your questions with short answers (see Game 1 for procedures):

am	am not				
are	aren't	do	don't	have	haven't
is	isn't	does	doesn't	has	hasn't
was	wasn't	did	didn't	had	hadn't
were	weren't				

will	won't	can	can't	may	may not
would	wouldn't	could	couldn't	should	shouldn't

COMPOUND SENTENCE BINGO

for High Beginning Students

LESSON: Find two people in the class who have the same number of sisters or brothers and two people who don't have any. Sum up the situation like this:

> Cesar has three brothers, and Susana *does too.*
>
> Cesar has three brothers, but Martin *doesn't.*
>
> Martin doesn't have any brothers, and Marco *doesn't either.*
>
> Martin doesn't have any brothers, but Susana *does.*

Similarly, find two people from the same country and two others from other countries:

> Leo is from Russia, and Boris *is too.*
>
> Leo is from Russia, but Lisa *isn't.*
>
> Lisa isn't from Nicaragua, and Leo *isn't either.*
>
> Lisa isn't from Nicaragua, but Laura *is.*

Now find two people who can swim (or sing, or ride a motorcycle, or cook, or some other common activity) and two others who cannot:

> Tran can swim, and Li *can too.*
>
> Tran can swim, but Jacques *can't.*
>
> Jacques can't swim, and Bok *can't either.*
>
> Jacques can't swim, but Tran *can.*

Finally, find two people who would like to go to a movie tonight (or stay in this country, or visit Russia this summer, or do some other activity) and two others who would not:

> Tella would like to see a movie tonight, and I *would too.*
>
> Tella would like to see a movie tonight, but Maria *wouldn't.*
>
> Maria wouldn't like to see a movie tonight, and Tam *wouldn't either.*
>
> Maria wouldn't like to see a movie tonight, but I *would.*

When the students seem to have caught on aurally to these structures, give them a written exercise similar to this one (using your own students' names and information):

COMPOUND SENTENCES with *TOO/EITHER, AND/BUT*

1. Cesar has two brothers, and Susana _____.

2. Cesar has two brothers, but Martin _____.

3. Martin doesn't have any brothers, and Marco _____.

4. Martin doesn't have any brothers, but Susana _____.

5. Leo is from Russia, and Boris _____.

6. Leo is from Russia, but Lisa _____.

7. Lisa isn't from Nicaragua, and Leo _____.

8. Lisa isn't from Nicaragua, but Laura _____.

9. Tran can swim, and Li _____.

10. Tran can swim, but Jacques _____.

11. Jacques can't swim, and Bok _____.

12. Jacques can't swim, but Tran _____.

13. Tella would like to see a movie tonight, and I _____.

14. Tella would like to see a movie tonight, but Maria _____.

15. Maria wouldn't like to see a movie tonight, and Tam _____.

16. Maria wouldn't like to see a movie tonight, but I _____.

Now try similar exercises with different auxiliaries:

Hugo *is* hungry, and I _____.

Mai *was* absent yesterday, but you _____.

Mohammed *should* stay home tomorrow, but Ivan _____.

Marie *shouldn't* work so hard, but Stephen _____.

We *were* cold last night, and you _____.

Dasam *may* eat chicken tonight, and I _____.

Lei *couldn't* understand any English last year, but Ti _____.

We *didn't* come to class yesterday, and they _____.

You*'re* hungry, and I _____.

SET-UP: Select just four of the auxiliaries your students are familiar with. Orally repeat sentences like the ones in the exercises on the previous page one more time, using the four selected auxiliaries. Pause after the second subject (where the blank is, in the written exercise), giving the students time to complete it. When they do, write the completion on the board. Repeat this with each of the four possible completions for each of the four selected auxiliaries. For example, if you use the four auxiliaries in the numbered exercise on the previous page, you will end up with this on the board:

does Too	doesn'T	doesn'T either	does
is Too	isn'T	isn'T either	is
can Too	can'T	can'T either	can
would Too	wouldn'T	wouldn'T either	would

PREPARATION: Give each student a 4x4 Bingo grid. Point out that there are 16 squares on their Bingo grids and 16 sentence completions on the chalkboard. Point to one of the completions and tell them to copy it into one of the squares. After allowing enough time for everyone to do this, point to a second completion and tell them to copy it into another square. Tell them that for Bingo everyone needs to have a different order, so urge them not to copy them all in the order they see on the board.

One student's grid may look like this:

does Too	isn'T either	would	can'T
isn'T	wouldn'T either	doesn'T	can Too
wouldn'T	does	can	is Too
is	doesn'T either	can'T either	would Too

While the students are preparing their grids, give each student some markers.

EXPLAIN THE GAME: (Suggested script:) **I'm going to begin a sentence such as, "Miguel lives in San Francisco, and Lamar [pause] ." Don't say anything! Find the correct completion on your paper and put a marker on it. When you have 4 squares in a row with markers, say "Bingo!" They can be horizontal, like this, or vertical, like this, or diagonal, like this. The first person to say Bingo and is correct is the winner. The second person is—too late!**

Repeat any of this that is not clear. Try as many examples as necessary to check everyone's comprehension of the procedures.

PLAY THE GAME: Scramble the 16 calling cards (provided) face down, then select one at random and begin any compound sentence *familiar to the students* which will elicit the completion you have drawn.

After giving the students ample time to find the correct square on their Bingo grids, set the calling card aside and select another one.

Continue selecting, eliciting, and setting aside the calling cards until someone says "Bingo!" If no one says *Bingo*, but you notice that someone has four marked squares in a row, point this out and coach them to say *Bingo!*

CHECK FOR CORRECT RESPONSES: Have the potential winner read the four winning squares to you.

Check them against the cards you have called and set aside. If all four squares are correct, give the winner a prize. Have everyone clear their grids of markers and begin again. "New game!"

If the four squares do not all match the items you have called, announce that there is "No Bingo!—Let's continue!"

Note: Do not reveal *which* of their completions is not correct because then other students will begin rearranging their markers according to this information and at least one person, but probably several, will come up with a winning combination without having identified the correct responses legitimately.

So make a point of listening to all four of the potential winner's answers *before* declaring that there is "No Bingo!" And when the students ask, "Which one is not correct?" say that you can't tell them that.

COMPOUND SENTENCE BINGO
for Intermediate Students and Advanced Students

This game is very similar to the previous one but instead of practicing

	(I am) **too**	and	(he won't) **either**,
it practices the use of	**so** (am I)	and	**neither** (will he).

LESSON: The lesson is exactly the same as the previous one, except that the *so/neither* endings replace the *too/either* endings, and several more auxiliaries can be added at these more advanced levels. (How many and which ones will depend on which verb tenses and modal auxiliaries your students are familiar with. See the calling cards provided with this book for a complete list of sentence completions which would be appropriate for this lesson.)

The lesson is repeated here with the *so/neither* variation for your convenience:

Find two people in the class who have the same number of sisters or brothers and two people who don't have any. Sum up (orally only at this point) the situation like this:

Cesar has two sisters, and *so does Susana.*

Cesar has two sisters, but *Martin doesn't.**

Martin doesn't have any sisters, and *neither does Marco.*

Martin doesn't have any sisters, but *Susana does.**

*Hopefully, at this level of English acquisition the difference between *and* and *but* is clear. It may still be useful, however, to contrast the two concepts in this context, as students struggling with the new *so/neither* endings typically go overboard and begin applying them in inappropriate places, such as compound sentences with *but* (Cesar has two sisters, but Martin doesn't either. or Martin doesn't have any sisters, but Susana does too.) Mixing Contrast Compounds (with *but*) together with Additional Compounds (with *and*) will provide the reminder that may be needed. If this part of the lesson seems to be superfluous for your students, however, it can be quickly dropped from both the remainder of the lesson as well as from the ensuing game(s).

Similarly, find two people from the same country and two others from other countries:

> Leo is from the Philippines, and *so is Nick.*
> Leo is from the Philippines, but Lisa *isn't.**
> Lisa isn't from Mexico, and *neither is Leo.*
> Lisa isn't from Mexico, but Laura *is.**

Now find two people who can sing (or swim, or ride a motorcycle, or cook, or some other common activity) and two others who cannot:

> Tran can sing, and *so can Li.*
> Tran can sing, but Jacques *can't.**
> Jacques can't sing, and *neither can Bok.*
> Jacques can't sing, but Tran *can.**

Finally, find two people who would like to go to summer school (or stay in this country, or go to a movie tonight, or do some other activity) and two others who would not:

> Tella would like to go to summer school, and *so would you.*
> Tella would like to go to summer school, but Maria *wouldn't.**
> Maria wouldn't like to go to summer school, and *neither would Tam.*
> Maria wouldn't like to go to summer school, but *you would.**

When the students seem to have caught on aurally to these structures, give them a written exercise similar to the one on the following page (using your students' names and information:)

COMPOUND SENTENCES with *SO/NEITHER, (AND/BUT)*

1. Cesar has two brothers, and _____ Susana.

2. Cesar has two brothers, but Martin _____ .

3. Martin doesn't have any brothers, and _____ Marco.

4. Martin doesn't have any brothers, but Susana _____ .

5. Leo is from Russia, and _____ Boris.

6. Leo is from Russia, but Lisa _____ .

7. Lisa isn't from Nicaragua, and _____ Leo.

8. Lisa isn't from Nicaragua, but Laura _____ .

9. Tran can swim, and _____ Li.

10. Tran can swim, but Jacques _____ .

11. Jacques can't swim, and _____ Bok.

12. Jacques can't swim, but Tran _____ .

13. Tella would like to see a movie tonight, and _____ you.

14. Tella would like to see a movie tonight, but Maria _____ .

15. Maria wouldn't like to see a movie tonight, and _____ Tam .

16. Maria wouldn't like to see a movie tonight, but I _____ .

Now try similar exercises with different auxiliaries:

Hugo *is* hungry, and _____ I.

Mai *was* absent yesterday, but you _____ .

Mohammed *should* stay home tomorrow, but Ivan _____ .

Marie *shouldn't* work so hard, but Stephen _____ .

We *were* cold last night, and _____ you.

Dasam *will* eat chicken tonight and _____ Amir.

Lei *couldn't* understand any English last year, but Ti _____ .

We *didn't* come to class yesterday, and _____ they.

You*'re* hungry, and _____ Maria.

They *haven't* eaten lunch yet, and _____ Synon.

SET-UP: Select just one person (I, you, Javier, Camar, it, we, they, etc.) and four of the auxiliaries your students are familiar with, or eight auxiliaries if you are not including the *but* compounds in your game (see * on page 106). It is, of course, possible to use more auxiliaries—if you're using 5x5 Bingo grids instead of 4x4s, or if you don't mind having students select just 16 (for 4x4s) or 25 (for 5x5s) endings from a larger selection of endings, so that no one student would have all the endings on their grid.

Orally repeat sentences like the ones in the exercises on the previous page one more time, now using *only* the selected person and the selected auxiliaries. Pause after the word *and* (or *but*, if you're using that variation), giving the students time to complete it orally. When they do, write the completion on the board. Repeat this with each of the two or four possible completions for each of the selected auxiliaries.

For example, if you use the first person singular *I* and the four auxiliaries in the numbered exercise on the previous page, you will end up with this on the board:

so do I	I don't	neither do I	I do
so am I	I'm not	neither am I	I am
so can I	I can't	neither can I	I can
so would I	I wouldn't	neither would I	I would

If, for another example, you don't include the *but* endings, and the auxiliaries you're using are *is, was, has, will, would, can, could,* and *should* with the name of one of the students, you will end up with something like this on the board:

so is Anna	neither is Anna
so was Anna	neither was Anna
so has Anna	neither has Anna
so will Anna	neither will Anna
so would Anna	neither would Anna
so can Anna	neither can Anna
so could Anna	neither could Anna
so should Anna	neither should Anna

PREPARATION: Give each student a Bingo grid. Point out the number of squares on the grids (16 or 25) and the number of sentence completions on the chalkboard. If there are more sentence completions than grid squares, tell them to select just 16 (or 25) of the sentence completions to copy onto their grids. Tell them to copy one completion into each square but not to copy them in the order they see on the board because this is for Bingo and everyone needs to have a *different* order.

One student's grid may look like this:

so could Anna	neither would Anna	so was Anna	neither will Anna
neither could Anna	so has Anna	neither was Anna	neither is Anna
so would Anna	neither can Anna	so is Anna	neither should Anna
so should Anna	so will Anna	so can Anna	neither has Anna

While the students are preparing their grids, give each student some markers.

EXPLAIN THE GAME: (Suggested script:) **I'm going to begin a sentence such as, "Miguel lives in San Francisco, and [pause] ." Don't say anything! Find the correct completion on your paper and put a marker on it. When you have 4 squares in a row with markers, say "Bingo!" They can be horizontal, like this, or vertical, like this, or diagonal, like this. The first person to say *Bingo* and is correct is the winner. The second person is—too late!**

Repeat any of this that is not clear. Try as many examples as necessary to check everyone's comprehension of the procedures.

PLAY THE GAME: Scramble the calling cards (provided) face down, then select one at random and begin any compound sentence *familiar to the students* which will elicit the completion you have drawn.

After giving the students ample time to find the correct square on their Bingo grids, set the calling card aside and select another one.

Continue selecting, eliciting, and setting aside the calling cards until someone says "Bingo!" If no one says *Bingo*, but you notice that someone has four marked squares in a row, point this out and coach them to say *Bingo*!

CHECK FOR CORRECT RESPONSES: Have the potential winner read the four winning squares to you.

Check them against the cards you have called and set aside. If all four squares are correct, give the winner a prize. Have everyone clear their grids of markers and begin again. "New game!"

If the four squares do not all match the items you have called, announce that there is "No Bingo!—Let's continue!"

Note: Do not reveal *which* of their completions is not correct because then other students will begin rearranging their markers according to this information and at least one person, but probably several, will come up with a winning combination without having identified the correct responses legitimately.

So make a point of listening to all four of the potential winner's answers *before* declaring that there is "No Bingo!" And when the students ask, "Which one is not correct?" say that you can't tell them that.

SECTION THREE
PHONOLOGY
BINGO

INTRODUCTION

Okay, now for the fun part!

The following 28 Bingo games deal with phonological or sound discriminations which certain language groups find troublesome to hear and/or pronounce. Mastery of these differences is not always necessary in order for an individual to comprehend English aurally or to be understood orally. Usually context and correct intonation will provide enough cues for communication.

However, most new speakers of English will appreciate having at least some rudimentary information about the phonemes that may at some point cause them trouble. If they are forewarned, for example, that there are two different sounds in the words *fill* and *feel,* then when they come across a problem where the two words are confused for some reason, they will know the *source* of the confusion and will be able to use spelling or writing to clarify which word is meant even if they cannot actually hear or pronounce the difference.

What follows are general instructions for all 28 games in this section. Additional, more specific notes precede each game. **Please be sure to read the notes for any game you plan to play with your class.** These include suggestions for **props** you may want to bring to class to make something clearer to your students. Most also point out at least one sentence in the game so simple and basic that you may use it as a gauge of the appropriateness of the game for the level of the students in your class. Look for this note: **"If your students don't understand this sentence, this game is too advanced for them. It would be better to do something else."**

Note: The author welcomes suggestions for improvements of any of these games in the form of simplifications of, or replacements for, sentences using the minimal pairs.

Information is also gladly accepted about which language groups have problems with each pair. The lists at the beginning of each game are by no means exhaustive and this author does not have experience with all of the languages listed. Much of the information in these lists was obtained from *Pronunciation Contrasts In English* by Don L. F. Nilsen and Alleen Pace Nilsen (Englewood Cliffs, NJ: Prentice Hall Regents, 1971).

Also welcome are proposals for additional pairs that give some ESL students trouble.

Please send any suggestions to this email address: **consee@aol.com**.

GENERAL INSTRUCTIONS
FOR ALL LESSONS IN THIS SECTION

TIME ALLOTMENT: Allow about 30 minutes for the lesson and preparation of any of these games (more time for less advanced students, less time for more advanced levels). Additionally, allow at least 10 minutes but not more than 25 minutes to *play* the game several times. Less than ten minutes will not be enough time to play more than two or three times, and that probably won't feel like all the preparation was quite worth the bother. On the other hand, more than 25 minutes of playing the game over and over may get rather tedious. Altho students generally don't get bored with these games, they can get *deadly* boring for the teacher!

LESSON: Write on separate parts of the chalkboard the spelling most common to each of the two or three phonemes featured in the game. For example, for the ĭ/ē game, these would be *i* and *ee*. Under the *i* write one of the words from the game containing this sound, for example *slip*. Under the *ee* write the corresponding word containing this sound, in this case *sleep*.

Discuss the meanings of the two words. Pronounce the two *sounds* in isolation (pointing to the letters) and then point to and pronounce the two *words* several times to allow students to clearly hear the contrast in pronunciation. Be sure that your pronunciation is loud and clear. Raising your pitch may help. If necessary, *exaggerate* the difference until the students catch on to it, but then return to a more *normal* pronunciation.

Now write an additional pair of words from the game, such as *live* and *leave* under the ones already on the chalkboard, so that you have the beginnings of a list of words under each sound. Briefly discuss the meanings of the two new words.

Note: The illustrations accompanying each game are intended to assist with the clarification of the meanings of the words and sentences. Please be sure to show these to the students whenever needed. Some sentences will be much easier for the students to understand, however, if you bring in some props. Suggestions for props are included in the notes preceding each game.

Warning: Do not use any game with any students whose level of English comprehension is too low to easily understand most of the sentences in the game. If the students learn a *little* new vocabulary, that's fine. But if there are too many new vocabulary items or if the language in general is too complicated for the students, the entire exercise will be completely lost on them. Drilling the sound discriminations alone, without any context, is not enough purpose for an ESL exercise. If there is no context, there is very little comprehension. If there is no comprehension, there is no communication. If there is no communication, then why would the exercise be used in a language classroom?

Next ask the students to point to the word or sound that you pronounce. Standing between the two lists, but looking out at the class, pronounce one of the items of either list. After a few students point to one side of the board or the other (they are all *supposed* to, but it may take a few tries to engage the whole class), point to the item you just pronounced.

Repeat several times, pronouncing and then pointing to a different item each time, and selecting as randomly as you can from one list or the other. (Don't be obvious by switching from one list to the other *every* time or by providing them with other cues such as a change in your intonation *only* when you switch lists. The only cue they should be getting is the difference in pronunciation between the two lists.)

Continue adding pairs of words to the lists in this manner until you have written on the board all eight minimal pairs (or, in the case of *kiss/keys*, *near* minimal pairs) featured in the selected game. The chalkboard for the ĭ/ē game will look something like this:

i	ee
slip	sleep
live	leave
his	he's
ship	sheep
kiss	keys
hit	heat
pill	peel
fill	feel

Of course, if the game you are using contrasts three phonemes instead of only two, you would make *three* lists on the board.

SET-UP: Distribute copies of the game to each student. Read the first pair of sentences (numbers 1 and 2). Have the students repeat the sentences. Discuss the meaning of anything that's not clear.

Now tell the students to listen to your pronunciation of the first part of one of the sentences and to tell you the correct ending. For example, in the ĭ/ē game, "I don't want you to sleep on the [pause]. *Sofa?* or *banana?* Which ending is correct? Yes, *sofa* is correct. Listen again." Repeat several times, sometimes using *slip* and sometimes using *sleep*.

As with the words on the board before, don't be obvious by switching from one sentence to the other *every* time or by providing them with other cues such as a change in your intonation *only* when you switch sentences. The only cue the students should be getting is the difference in pronunciation between the two words, in this case *slip* and *sleep*.

Continue this listening, repeating, sentence completion/sound discrimination practice with the remaining seven pairs of sentences in the game.

PREPARATION: Give each student a 4x4 Bingo grid. Show them that there are 16 squares on their Bingo grids and 16 sentences on the paper. Tell them to copy the *endings only* of the 16 sentences into the 16 squares of the Bingo grid.

It's important not to copy them in order, so that each person will have a *different* order.

As the students prepare their grids, you can hand out bingo markers to each student.

EXPLAIN THE GAME: (Suggested script:) **I'm going to read one of the sentences, for example, "I don't want you to slip on the [pause]" Don't *say* anything! Just put a marker on the correct ending on your paper. When you have 4 squares in a row with markers, say, "Bingo!" They can be horizontal, like this, or vertical, like this, or diagonal, like this. The first person to say *Bingo* and is correct is the winner. The second person is—too late!**

Repeat any of this that is not clear. Try as many examples as necessary to check everyone's comprehension of the procedures and to drill the sound differences a few more times.

PLAY THE GAME: Scramble the 16 call numbers (provided) face down, then select one at random and read the corresponding sentence, pausing instead of reading the ending. (You may have to say *shhh!* a few times in place of the ending to remind students not to give away the answer: "I don't want you to slip on the shhh!" [with forefinger to lips])

After giving the students enough time to find the correct sentence on their papers and then the correct ending on their Bingo grids, place the call number next to its sentence on your copy of the game, and select another call number.

Note: For these games, do *not* continue selecting call numbers *completely* at random. It's a good idea to avoid calling both items of a contrasting pair or trio, if possible. If, for example, #4 has already been drawn, then if #3 (which contrasts with #4) comes up, set it aside *without* calling it until one of each contrasting pair has been drawn. If no one achieves Bingo after these first 8 (one of each pair) *then* go back and call the others until someone says Bingo. Why? Whenever both #3 and #4 are called, the students may mark #3 for #4 and vice versa, thereby possibly getting Bingo without having heard either item correctly. This, of course, defeats the whole purpose of the game.

Continue selecting, reading, and placing the call numbers on your paper until someone says "Bingo!" If no one says *Bingo*, but you notice that someone has four marked squares in a row, point this out and coach them to say *Bingo*!

CHECK FOR CORRECT RESPONSES: Have the potential winner read the four winning squares to you. Check them against the call numbers you have called and placed next to the corresponding sentences of the illustrated sheet. If all four squares are correct, give the winner a prize. Have everyone clear their grids of markers and begin again. "New game!"

If the four squares do *not* all match the items you have called, announce that there is "No Bingo!—Let's continue!"

Note: Do not reveal *which* of their answers is not correct because then other students will begin rearranging their markers according to this information, and at least one person, but probably several, will come up with a winning combination without having identified the correct endings themselves.

So make a point of listening to all four of the potential winner's answers *before* declaring that there is "No Bingo!" And when the students ask, "Which one is not correct?" say that you can't tell them that.

ă/ŏ/ŭ Bingo Notes

Some language groups prone to problems discriminating between at least two of these three sounds: Arabic, Burmese, Cantonese, Cebuano, Croatian, Czech, Danish, Fijian, Georgian, German, Greek, Hausa, Hawaiian, Hebrew, Indonesian, Italian, Japanese, Mandarin, Micronesian, Navajo, Pashto, Persian, Polish, Protuguese, Russian, Samoan, Serbian, Spanish, Swedish, Tagalog, Telugu, Tongan, Turkish, Urdu.

Suggestions for clarification of the meanings of the sentences in this game:

1, 2, 3. Refer to the pictures.

4, 5. Refer to the picture of the *poppies* and the *puppies* on the cover of the book. Better yet, bring a photo of some poppies.

6.   Refer to the picture of the *cat*, or bring in a soft toy cat*.

7, 8. Refer to the picture of the man on a *cot* with a *cat* and a *cut* leg.

9, 11. Point out that *ran* is the past form of *run*. (Demonstrate running if necessary.)

10. Have three students stand up. Tell one to imagine that the second one is her cousin named *Ron* and that the third is her cousin named *Bob*. Now point to them one by one as you tell her, "You, Ron, and Bob are cousins."

12. Suggested prop*: a street *map* of the town you are in.

13-16. Refer to the pictures.

*****Note**:   The more advanced your students, the less need there is for props (but it's still a lot of fun to use them.)

ă/ŏ/ŭ Bingo

1. I can see their **backs**   but not their faces.
2. I can see their **box**   of money.
3. I can see their **bucks**   in their pockets.

4. The **poppies** are   pink.
5. The **puppies** are   brown.

6. The **cat** is   very soft.
7. The **cot** is   uncomfortable.
8. The **cut** is   painful.

9. You **ran**   to school last Monday.
10. You, **Ron**   and Bob are cousins.
11. You **run**   to school every morning.

12. We used the **map**   to find the street.
13. We used the **mop**   to clean the floor.

14. The **cap** is   on your head.
15. The **cop** is   angry.
16. The **cup** is   for your coffee.

Puppies Or Poppies? ESL Bingo   ©1998 Elizabeth Kuizenga Romijn, Command Performance (510) 524-1191

ă/ĕ/ĭ Bingo Notes

Some language groups prone to problems discriminating between at least two of these three sounds: Arabic, Bulgarian, Burmese, Cantonese, Cebuano, Croatian, Czech, Dutch, Fijian, Finnish, Georgian, German, Greek, Gujarati, Hawaiian, Hebrew, Hindi, Hmong, Hungarian, Indonesian, Italian, Japanese, Javanese, Korean, Mandarin, Marshallese, Micronesian, Navajo, Norwegian, Pashto, Persian, Polish, Portuguese, Russian, Samoan, Serbian, Spanish, Swahili, Swedish, Tagalog, Tamil, Telugu, Thai, Tongan, Turkish, Urdu, Uzbek, Vietnamese.

Suggestions for clarification of the meanings of the sentences in this game:

1. Refer to the picture.

2. *Pantomime* signing your name with a *pen*.

3. Refer to the picture of the jeans with a safety *pin* holding a hole closed. Suggested props*: various kinds of *pins*: safety pin, straight pin (dressmaker's), lapel pin (jewelry).

4. On the board, *draw* a stick figure of one *man*. Label it *man*.

5. *Draw* several stick figures of *men*. Label them *men*. Have the students listen to your pronunciation of *man* and *men* and point to the correct stick figures as you do.

6, 8. Refer to the picture of people *lifting* weights and *laughing (at jokes)*.

7. Point out that *left* is the past form of *leave*. If your students don't know this meaning of the word *leave,* demonstrate leaving your wallet at "home" (a designated area of the classroom).**

9-11. Refer to the pictures.

12. Suggested prop*: a *bell* with a clear sound.

13. Suggested prop*: a very high telephone *bill* or utility bill.

14, 15. If your students don't understand these two definitions, this game is too advanced for them. It would be better to do something else.

16. Demonstrate hiding something.**

---

*Note: The more advanced your students, the less need there is for props (but it's still a lot of fun to use them.)

**Note: Sometimes it's more efficient and just as productive to ***translate*!

ă/ĕ/ĭ Bingo

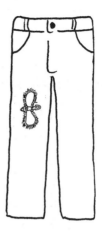

1. I used a **pan** to  cook my dinner.

2. I used a **pen** to sign my name.

3. I used a **pin** to close the hole.

4. The **man** is here.

5. The **men** are here.

6. We **laughed** at the funny jokes.

7. We **left** our money at home.

8. We **lift** weights for exercise.

9. You need some **jam** and bread.

10. You need some **gem** stones.

11. You need some **gym** equipment.

12. The **bell** has a beautiful sound.

13. The **bill** — is very high.

14. **Had—** the past form of have

15. **Head—** on top of your neck

16. **Hid—** the past form of hide

Puppies Or Poppies? ESL Bingo ©1998 Elizabeth Kuizenga Romijn, Command Performance (510) 524-1191

ĕ/ā Bingo Notes

Some language groups prone to problems discriminating between these two sounds:
Arabic, Cantonese, Cebuano, Fijian, French, Georgian, Greek, Hebrew, Indonesian, Italian, Japanese, Korean, Mandarin, Micronesian, Navajo, Pashto, Samoan, Swahili, Tagalog, Tamil, Telugu, Thai, Tongan, Turkish, Urdu, Uzbek, Vietnamese.

Suggestions for clarification of the meanings of the sentences in this game:

1. Suggested prop*: a towel or small bed sheet, folded up to begin with. Demonstrate putting it on "the bed" (or table) folded up, and then unfolding it and *spreading* it on the same object. A *sheet* is a cover for a bed, the one that is easy to wash that goes under the other covers.

2. Suggested prop*: a spray bottle of water. You may spray water on a sheet before ironing it.

3. Someone in your class must have a *pen* in their *pocket* or at least a pocket where you can put a pen.

4. Put your hand on your neck and wince as if you are in *pain*.

5. *Test* in this case is a verb meaning *to give a test.*

6. The verb *taste* means to try to eat a little bit to see if you like the flavor.

7, 8. Refer to the pictures.

9. The *lens* of eyeglasses is the glass part that corrects your vision.

10. Refer to the picture to point out the *lanes* of the road.

11. This means it rained for a long time during the winter—lots of water from early winter until late winter.

12. They had to wait for a long time.

13. A *debt* is something you have to pay because you borrowed it or you bought something or received some service and you haven't paid for it yet.**

14. A *date* is similar to an *appointment*, but an appointment is for business and a date is for fun or pleasure. A *date* with her boyfriend is probably something romantic— to go out to dinner or to the movies or to go dancing or to a party.

15. Point out the *edge* of a table in your classroom. (Better yet, make it dirty first.) Then point out the edges of other things in the room, e.g., the chalkboard, the door, the wastebasket, a book, a piece of paper, the shirt you're wearing.

16. The *age* of the table refers to *how old* it is.

Note: The more advanced your students, the less need there is for props (but it's still a lot of fun to use them.)

Note: Sometimes it's more efficient and just as productive to ***translate*!

ĕ/ā Bingo

1. I **spread** the sheet   on the bed.

2. I **sprayed** the sheet   with water.

3. He has a **pen** in his   pocket.

4. He has a **pain** in his   neck.

5. We will **test** the new   students.

6. We will **taste** the new   ice cream.

7. The long **bread** is   on the table.

8. The long **braid** is   down her back.

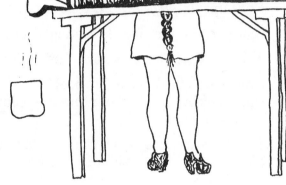

9. Can you fix the **lens** of   my glasses?

10. Can you fix the **lanes** of   the road?

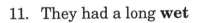

11. They had a long **wet**   winter.

12. They had a long **wait**   for the bus.

13. She has a **debt**   she can't pay.

14. She has a **date**   with her boyfriend.

15. The **edge** of the table is   dirty.

16. The **age** of the table is   300 years.

ĭ/ē Bingo Notes

Some language groups prone to problems discriminating between these two sounds:
Arabic, Bulgarian, Burmese, Cantonese, Cebuano, Croatian, Estonian, Fijian, French, Georgian, Greek, Haitian Creole, Hausa, Hawaiian, Hebrew, Hmong, Hungarian, Indonesian, Italian, Japanese, Korean, Laotian, Mandarin, Micronesian, Navajo, Persian, Portuguese, Russian, Samoan, Serbian, Spanish, Swahili, Swedish, Tagalog, Tamil, Thai, Tongan, Turkish, Urdu, Vietnamese.

Suggestions for clarification of the meanings of the sentences in this game:

1. *Pantomime slipping* on a banana. Also refer to the picture.

2. Refer to the picture of the dog *sleeping* on the sofa.

3. Ask some students where they *lived* last year to check comprehension.

4. *Demonstrate* leaving a book in an out-of-the-way place, then forgetting where, then looking for it. Then become someone else asking the question, "Where did you *leave* your book?"**

5, 6. If your students don't understand these two sentences, this game is too advanced for them. It would be better to do something else.

7, 8. Refer to the pictures.

9, 10. If you've already discussed the meanings of the words *kiss* and *keys,* your students will understand these sentences. See 5,6.

11. *Pantomime* the meaning of *hitting* (without hurting or frightening anyone, of course.)**

12. *Pantomime heating* some soup on the stove. Suggested props*: soup can, small sauce pan, a book or rack or box to use as a stove. See page 31 of *Live Action English (Romijn & Seely, Berkeley: Command Performance Language Institute, 1997)* for a complete TPR soup-heating sequence.

13. Suggested props*: vitamin C bottle and a variety of pills or M&M's, one of them orange.

14. Suggested prop*: an orange—*demonstrate* peeling it and throwing the peel in the garbage. See page 44 of *Live Action English (Romijn & Seely, Berkeley: Command Performance Language Institute, 1997)* for a complete TPR orange-peeling sequence.

15. *Fill out* an application means *complete* an application.

16. If your students don't understand this question, this game is too advanced for them. It would be better to do something else.

*Note: The more advanced your students, the less need there is for props (but it's still a lot of fun to use them.)

Note: Sometimes it's more efficient and just as productive to ***translate!*

ĭ/ē Bingo

1. I don't want you to **slip** on the   banana.
2. I don't want you to **sleep** on the   sofa.

3. Where did you **live**   last year?
4. Where did you **leave**   your book?

5. **His**   mother is sick.
6. **He's**   a good student.

7. The **ship** is in the   ocean.
8. The **sheep** is in the   barn.

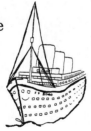

9. He gave her the **kiss**   because he loves her.
10. He gave her the **keys**   to his car.

11. I saw her **hit** the   dog.
12. I saw her **heat** the   soup.

13. The orange **pill** is   Vitamin C.
14. The orange **peel** is   in the garbage.

15. How do you **fill**   out an application?
16. How do you **feel**   today?

Puppies Or Poppies? ESL Bingo ©1998 Elizabeth Kuizenga Romijn, Command Performance (510) 524-1191

ā/ē/ī Bingo Notes

> **Note:** Altho these three *sounds* are difficult for very few ESL/EFL students, speakers of other languages which use the Roman alphabet often have trouble at first remembering *which letter* is pronounced *how*. Thanks to the Great Vowel Shift which took place in English several hundred years ago, our letter *a* is pronounced like their *e* plus a glide: *ey;* our *e* is pronounced like their *i* plus a glide: *iy*; and our *i* is pronounced like their *a* plus a glide: *ay*. Less literate students find this particularly confusing and benefit from the practice offered by this Bingo game.

Suggestions for clarification of the meanings of the sentences in this game:

1, 2, 3. If your students don't understand these three sentences, this game is too advanced for them. It would be better to do something else.

4, 5, 6. *Told* is the past form of *tell*. If your students still don't understand these 3 sentences, have one stand up. Identify another student as "May." Tell the person standing to tell May to come to school. Ask her if *you* can come to school, too. Tell her to tell you *no*. Now identify another student as your "sister". Ask if your sister can come to school. Tell her to tell your sister *yes*. Now recap what has just taken place: "You told May to come to school; you told me *no*; you told my sister *yes*."**

7, 8. Refer to the pictures of the *whale* and the *wheels* of various sizes.

9. *A little while longer* means *a short time (or a few minutes) more.*

10, 11, 12. Point out that gambling casinos are illegal in most states in the U.S. and refer to the picture of the mounted police *raid*ing an illegal casino. Note that one policeman is sitting in the casino *read*ing a newspaper.

13. Suggested prop*: a paintbrush of any kind. See page 18 of *Live Action English (Romijn & Seely, Berkeley: Command Performance Language Institute, 1997)* for a complete TPR picture-painting sequence.

14. Suggested prop*: a pint milk carton.

15, 16. *Demonstrate wiping* the table and *weeping* (crying quietly).

---

*Note: The more advanced your students, the less need there is for props (but it's still a lot of fun to use them.)

Note: Sometimes it's more efficient and just as productive to **translate!

ā/ē/ī Bingo

1. **A** is the first letter of the word   America.
2. **E** is the first letter of the word   English.
3. **I** is the first letter of the word   India.

4. You told **May**   to come to school.
5. You told **me**   NO.
6. You told **my**   sister YES.

7. I'm waiting for a little **whale**   to eat this fish.

8. I'm waiting for a little **wheel**   for my bike.

9. I'm waiting for a little **while**   longer.

10. The police will **raid**   the casino.
11. The police will **read**   the newspaper.
12. The police will **ride**   horses.

13. Do you have a **paint**   brush?
14. Do you have a **pint**   of milk?

15. My mother is **weeping**   because she's sad.
16. My mother is **wiping**   the table.

ŏ/ar/er Bingo Notes

> **Some language groups prone to problems discriminating between these two sounds:**
> Cantonese

Suggestions for clarification of the meanings of the sentences in this game:

1. Demonstrate putting the *dot* on an *i.*

2. Refer to the picture of the target and the *dart.*

3. Refer to the picture of the shovel full of earth on the ground (in front of the truck).

4. If your students don't understand this sentence, this game is too advanced for them. It would be better to do something else.

5. *Having the heart* to do something means *feeling good* doing it. If "I don't have the heart to tell you what happened," that means I don't want to tell you what happened because you will not like to hear it and I don't want to make you sad.

6. Wrap someone's hand in a makeshift bandage as if it is hurt. Who has a hurt hand? Not me. My hand isn't hurt. I don't have the hurt hand. *She* has the hurt hand.

7. Refer to the picture of the dog looking out the top of a *box* on the back of a truck.

8. Demonstrate the *bark* of an angry dog.

9. A *shock* is a *bad surprise.*

10. Refer to the picture of the shark in the water.

11, 12. Refer to the picture of the *barn* and cows. Also note the poor farmer who has burned his leg with a branding iron.

13. Point to the *far* corner (from you) in the classroom.

14. Refer to the picture of the rabbit. *Fur* is the name for a rabbit's *hair* (or any other soft animal: cat, mouse, dog, etc.)

15. Refer to the *clock* in the room.

16. The *clerk* is the person in the store who answers questions and takes your money when you pay.

ŏ/ar/er Bingo

1. Put the **dot** on the   letter *i*.

2. Put the **dart** on the target.

3. Put the **dirt** on the   ground.

4. I don't have the **hot**   dinner.

5. I don't have the **heart**   to tell you what happened.

6. I don't have the **hurt**   hand.

7. The dog **box**   is on the truck.

8. The dog **barks**   when he's angry.

9. It was a **shock**  to hear the news.

10. It was a **shark**   in the water.

11. Do you have a **barn**   for the cows?

12. Do you have a **burn**   on your leg?

13. Look at the **far**   corner.

14. Look at the **fur**   on the rabbit.

15. The **clock** can tell you   the time.

16. The **clerk** can tell you   how much to pay.

Puppies Or Poppies? ESL Bingo ©1998 Elizabeth Kuizenga Romijn, Command Performance (510) 524-1191

aw/or Bingo Notes

Some language groups prone to problems discriminating between these two sounds: Cantonese, Mandarin.

Suggestions for clarification of the meanings of the sentences in this game:

1. Refer to the picture of the *saw*. *Dull* is the opposite of *sharp*. Suggested props*: a dull knife (or scissors) and a sharp one, and something to cut with them.

2. Refer to the picture of the man trying to cut wood with a painful arm. Wince as you pretend that your own arm is *sore*.

3. *Caught* is the past form of *catch*. When you are late for the bus, sometimes you have to run to *catch* it. (Demonstrate)

4. In this case, *court* means *try to get someone to love you or marry you*. People in different countries do this in different ways. In some countries, people are not allowed to *court*; marriages are arranged by others.

5. Refer to the picture of the cat cleaning her feet *(paws)*. Yes, we use *he* and *she* for animals when we know their gender. The pronoun *it* is for *inanimate* objects, not for familiar animals.

6. Refer to the picture of the girl rubbing a small cloth on her face. The *pores* are the little holes in the skin.

7. A *flaw* is a *mistake* or *defect* or *imperfection*. Suggested prop*: a flawed photograph.

8. If your students don't understand this sentence, this game is too advanced for them. It would be better to do something else.

9. Ask a woman or girl in the class to *draw* a tree on the chalkboard. Tell everyone else to "watch her draw."

10. Refer to the picture of the open drawer. Note that *draw* in item 9 is a verb, or action word, and *drawer* in item 10 is a noun, the name of that part of the dresser.

11. Suggested props*: *raw* carrots to break while the students listen to the sound.

12. Suggested prop*: sound recording of a lion's *roar* or a picture of a lion roaring. You can find such a recording on the internet at:
    www.georgetown.edu/cball/animals/lion.au

13. Suggested prop*: any kind of *sauce* that could be used for chicken.

14. *Source* means *cause* or *reason* or *origin*.**

15, 16. Suggested prop*: a picture of soldiers fighting in a fortress. (Or maybe you can describe the scene to them.)

*Note: The more advanced your students, the less need there is for props (but it's still a lot of fun to use them.)

aw/or Bingo

1. I can't cut the wood with this **saw.**   It's dull.

2. I can't cut the wood with this **sore**   arm.

3. I don't know how they **caught**   the bus.

4. I don't know how they **court**   in their country.

5. She cleaned her **paws** with   her tongue.

6. She cleaned her **pores** with   alcohol.

7. He didn't see the **flaw** in my   photograph.

8. He didn't see the **floor** in my   kitchen.

9. Watch her **draw**   a picture of a tree.

10. Watch her **drawer**   when she opens it.

11. Listen to the **raw**   carrots break.

12. Listen to the **roar**   of the lion.

13. Here's the **sauce**   for the chicken.

14. Here's the **source**   of the problem.

15. What does *fought* mean?   The past form of *fight*.

16. What does *fort* mean?   A protected place for an army.

Puppies Or Poppies? ESL Bingo ©1998 Elizabeth Kuizenga Romijn, Command Performance (510) 524-1191

hV-/V- Bingo Notes

Some language groups prone to problems discriminating between an initial *h-* and an initial vowel: French, Haitian Creole, Italian, Portuguese, Russian, Spanish.

Suggestions for clarification of the meanings of the sentences in this game:

1. *Heat* means to *make it hot*. Demonstrate heating soup on a "stove" (a book or rack or box).** See page 31 of *Live Action English (Romijn & Seely, Berkeley: Command Performance Language Institute, 1997)* for a complete TPR soup-heating sequence.

2. Demonstrate eating soup with a spoon (refer to the picture).

3. Suggested prop:* plastic (or real) broccoli.

4. *Whole* means *all, everything, complete.*

5. Refer to the picture of the bald man.

6. Refer to the picture of the astronaut wearing an oxygen helmet on the moon.

7. You had a party? Why? I don't know *why* you had a party.

8. *Add* means *put in*. You like to put milk in your coffee. You like to *add* milk to your coffee. Why? I don't know why.

9. Take off your shoe and point out the *heel*. Point to some of the students' shoes and tell them to look at their heels.

10. Refer to the picture of the *eel*.

11. Refer to the picture of the people climbing a *hill*.

12. *Ill* means *sick*.

13, 14, 15, 16. If your students don't understand these four sentences with a little pointing to appropriate body parts, this game is too advanced for them. It would be better to do something else.

***Note:** The more advanced your students, the less need there is for props (but it's still a lot of fun to use them.)

****Note**: Sometimes it's more efficient and just as productive to ***translate***!

hV-/V- Bingo

1. Why don't you **heat** the soup   on the stove?
2. Why don't you **eat** the soup   with a spoon?

3. They really **hate**   broccoli.
4. They really **ate**   the whole cake.

5. There's no **hair**   on his head.

6. There's no **air**   on the moon.

7. I don't know why you **had**   a party.
8. I don't know why you **add**   milk to your coffee.

9. Look at the **heel**   of your shoe.
10. Look at the **eel**   in the water.

11. That's the **hill**   we like to climb.
12. That's the **ill**   old man.

13. He had a pain in his arm, **hand**   and shoulder.
14. He had a pain in his arm **and**   his neck.

15. I'm glad to see her **here**   at home.
16. I'm glad to see her **ear**   is better.

Intervocalic r/t Bingo Notes

Note: Altho these two *sounds* are not difficult for anyone to discriminate, speakers of other languages which use the Roman alphabet and/or have a "rolled r" often hear our intervocalic *t* (and *d*) as an *r* and tend to picture it that way before they see a word with it spelled out. Less literate students find this particularly confusing and benefit from the practice offered by this Bingo game.

Suggestions for clarification of the meanings of the sentences in this game:

1, 2. Act out the "introduction" to the class of your imaginary sister and brother, explaining that *Barry* is a man's name in English and *Betty* is a woman's name.

3. Cup your ear and tell the students to listen. When everyone is quiet, pick out a sound coming form outside that you hear clearly. For example, if you here traffic, ask, "Do you hear the traffic? *Can you hear it... outside?*"

4. Pantomime cooking something on an imaginary stove. *Heat* means *make it hot.*

5. Have one of the women in your class take off one *earring* and put it under her chair. Then ask, "Where's her earring? [pointing to it] I can see it under the chair! I can see her earring under the chair."

6. Now have her pantomime *eating* her lunch. Look out the window and pretend you see another student out the window. "Look, She's eating her lunch too. I can see *her* eating her lunch."

7, 8, 9. If your students don't understand these questions, this game is too advanced for them. It would be better to do something else.

10. Draw a strange or oversimplified flower on the board and ask, "What is it?" If no one can tell, explain, "It's a flower."

11, 12. *Demonstrate pouring* soup into a bowl and *putting* soup on the table.** Also refer to the illustration. See page 31 of *Live Action English (Romijn & Seely, Berkeley: Command Performance Language Institute, 1997)* for a complete TPR soup-serving sequence.

13, 14. Same as 7, 8, 9.

15, 16. Have a student spell (aloud) the names *Carrie* and *Katie* (while looking at the paper if necessary).

**Note: Sometimes it's more efficient and just as productive to translate!

r/t Bingo

1. I want you to meet **Barry**, my   brother.
2. I want you to meet **Betty**, my   sister.

3. Can you **hear it**   outside?
4. Can you **heat it**   on the stove?

5. I can see her **earring**   under the chair.
6. I can see her **eating**   her lunch.

7. **Where** are you   going?
8. **What** are you   doing?

9. **Where** is it?   Here it is!
10. **What** is it?   It's a flower.

11. He's **pouring** the soup   in the bowl.
12. He's **putting** the soup   on the table.

13. What is he **wearing**   today?
14. What is he **waiting**   for?

15. You're supposed to spell **Carrie** with   double **r**.
16. You're supposed to spell **Katie** with   a **t**.

r/l Bingo Notes

> **Some language groups prone to problems discriminating between these two sounds:** Burmese, Cantonese, Hawaiian, Hmong, Japanese, Korean, Micronesian, Samoan, Swahili, Thai, Vietnamese.

Suggestions for clarification of the meanings of the sentences in this game:

1, 2. If your students don't understand these sentences, this game is too advanced for them. It would be better to do something else.

3, 4. Refer to the picture of the *raspberries*, and the boy with a round *belly* eating from the bush.

5. Same as 1, 2.

6. Tell the students to imagine that each has an old bottle. Pantomime *collect*ing them all.

7. Refer to the *tires* on the picture of the car.

8. Refer to the picture of the step with decorative *tiles*.

9, 10. Same as 1, 2.

11. Refer to the picture of the woman pushing a lawn mower.

12. *Glass* is the material a window is made of. To make a window, it's necessary to cut a piece of glass the correct size for the window.

13. *Wrong* is the opposite of *right* or *correct*. In this case the color of the dress isn't good with the colors of other things around it.

14. Refer to the picture of the *long* black dress.

15, 16. Refer to the picture of the boy with *rice* and *lice*. Explain that *lice* are insects which like to live in people's hair.

r/l Bingo

1. Look at your **wrist**   watch.
2. Look at your **list**   of names.

3. He has a big **berry** from   the raspberry bush.
4. He has a big **belly** from   eating too much.

5. Please **correct** all the   mistakes.
6. Please **collect** all the   old bottles.

7. There are four **tires** on my   car.
8. There are four **tiles** on my   front step.

9. I'm going to **fry**   an egg.
10. I'm going to **fly**   to New York.

11. She cut the **grass**   in the front yard.
12. She cut the **glass**   for the window.

13. Your dress is the **wrong**   color.
14. Your dress is the **long**   black one.

15. He has **rice** in his   bowl.
16. He has **lice** in his   hair.

n/l Bingo Notes

Some language groups prone to problems discriminating between these two sounds: Cantonese, Estonian, Thai, Vietnamese.

Suggestions for clarification of the meanings of the sentences in this game:

1-2. *Dark* and *bright* are opposites. Refer to the picture of the bright light in the dark night.

3. Refer to picture of the movie ad.

4. Refer to picture of the *lotus* blossom.

5. Suggested prop:* a jacket or shirt with *snaps* for fasteners.

6. Demonstrate *slapping* cold water on your face.

7. Refer to the picture of the *bones* being thrown away.

8. A dishwasher can be a *machine* that washes dishes or a *person* who washes dishes. In this case, we know it's a machine because we put the *bowls inside*. Suggested prop:* a soup bowl.

9. Refer to the picture of the *train*.

10. Refer to the picture of the *trail* of foot prints.

11. Refer to the picture of the *spoon*.

12. Refer to the picture of the *spool of thread*, but better yet, bring in a spool of thread to show.*

13. Large cities have more than one post office. The *main* post office is the principle one or the central one. All the mail from the other post offices in the city is collected there before it is sent to other places.

14. Refer to the picture of the *mail box*.

15. Refer to the picture of the *pine tree* with a bag under it.

16. Refer to the picture of the *pile of rocks*.

---

*Note: The more advanced your students, the less need there is for props (but it's still a lot of fun to use them.)

n/l Bingo

1. The **night** is very   dark.
2. The **light** is very   bright.

3. Did you see the **notice**   about the new movie?

4. Did you see the **lotus**   flower?

5. In the morning I **snapped**   up my jacket.
6. In the morning I **slapped**   cold water on my face.

7. After lunch we put the **bones** in the   garbage.

8. After lunch we put the **bowls** in the   dishwasher.

9. We followed the **train**   to New York.
10. We followed the **trail**   of footprints.

11. I need a **spoon**   to eat my soup.
12. I need a **spool**   of thread.

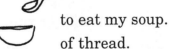

13. Take the letter to the **main**   post office.
14. Take the letter to the **mail**   box.

15. You can find the bag under a **pine**   tree.

16. You can find the bag under a **pile**   of rocks.

Puppies Or Poppies? ESL Bingo ©1998 Elizabeth Kuizenga Romijn, Command Performance (510) 524-1191

m/n/ng Bingo Notes

Some language groups prone to problems discriminating between at least two of these three sounds: Arabic, Bulgarian, Cantonese, Croatian, Czech, Estonian, French, Georgian, Greek, Hausa, Hawaiian, Hebrew, Hungarian, Italian, Japanese, Mandarin, Navajo, Persian, Polish, Portuguese, Polish, Russian, Samoan, Serbian, Shanghainese, Spanish, Telugu, Turkish, Urdu.

Suggestions for clarification of the meanings of the sentences in this game:

1. Refer to the picture of the *ham* and eggs breakfast.

2. Refer to the picture of the girl waving goodbye.

3. Refer to the picture of the coat *hang*ing on a chair.

4. Suggested prop:* *rum* bottle; *pantomime* drinking a bit very cautiously and then declaring that it's the first rum you've ever had.

5. Refer to the picture of the footrace.

6. Refer to the picture of the ladder (against the truck).

7. Suggested prop:* roll of *Tums*. Make it clear that you're not endorsing them!

8. Refer to the picture of a truck of sand at the beach.

9. Point to your *tongue*. Indicate that between you and two of the students, you have 3 *tongues*.

10. *Thin* is the opposite of *fat*. Point out the thin man at the beach.

11. If students are not sure what this means, remind them of something comical that has been said in your class today that made everyone laugh.

12. Refer to the picture of the girl and call her your daughter named *Kim*.

13. Bring a picture of an extended family that could be (or is) yours.*

14. Refer to the picture of the *king* counting his money.

15. Refer to the picture of the child (*Kim* from #12) playing with her chewing *gum*.

16. Refer to the picture of the person in the footrace pushing a *gun* away from herself.

*Note: The more advanced your students, the less need there is for props (but it's still a lot of fun to use them.)

m/n/ng Bingo

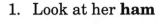

1. Look at her **ham**   and eggs.

2. Look at her **hand**   waving goodbye.

3. Look at her **hang**   her coat on the chair.

4. That's the first **rum**   I ever drank.

5. That's the first **run**   of the season.

6. That's the first **rung** of the ladder.

7. We have three **Tums**   for our stomachaches.

8. We have three **tons**   of sand from the beach.

9. We have three **tongues** to speak English.

10. That's a funny **thin**   man.

11. That's a funny **thing** to say.

12. My **Kim**    is a wonderful girl.

13. My **kin**   are my family.

14. My **king**   is very rich.

15. Keep the **gum**   in your mouth!

16. Keep the **gun** 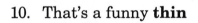   away from me!

Puppies Or Poppies? ESL Bingo   ©1998 Elizabeth Kuizenga Romijn, Command Performance (510) 524-1191

145

y/j Bingo Notes

> **Some language groups prone to problems discriminating between these two sounds:** Estonian, Finnish, Dutch, German, Greek, Hebrew, Indonesian, Micronesian, Norwegian, Persian, Portuguese, Spanish, Swahili, Swedish, Thai.

Suggestions for clarification of the meanings of the sentences in this game:

1. Suggested prop:* a *yam* (and any kind of *pie* to cut up for Bingo prizes).

2. Refer to the picture of *jam* and bread.

3. Suggested prop:* empty peanut butter *jar* with plastic (or real) bugs inside.

4. *Yard* is the area outside around your house.

5. *Yolk* is the yellow part of an egg.

6. Tell a story containing two *jokes* or ...**

7. Suggested prop:* empty *Jello* box, or some *Jello* made up. (Now winners can choose between a slice of yam pie and a scoop of Jello!) Make it clear that you're not endorsing the Jello.

8. If your students don't understand this sentence, this game is too advanced for them. It would be better to do something else.

9. That radio is no good. It's broken. I don't need it.**

10. For example, orange *juice*.

11. Refer to a calendar showing *July* before August.

12. *You lie!* means *I don't believe you; that's not true.* **

13, 14. Pretend you are waiting for someone at the airport. Ask these two questions, referring to the picture of the people coming off the jet.

15, 16. *Demonstrate* stretching, yawning, getting up, doing exercises. See page 14 of *Live Action English (Romijn & Seely, Berkeley: Command Performance Language Institute, 1997)* for a complete TPR morning routine sequence.

*****Note**: The more advanced your students, the less need there is for props (but it's still a lot of fun to use them.)

******Note**: Sometimes it's more efficient and just as productive to ***translate*!**

y/j Bingo

1. For lunch we had soup and **yam**   pie.
2. For lunch we had soup and **jam**   on bread.

3. There are bugs in the **yard**   behind my house.
4. There are bugs in the **jar**   of peanut butter.

5. There are two **yolks** in that   egg.
6. There are two **jokes** in that   story.

7. We're going to have **yellow**   flowers for the party.
8. We're going to have **Jello**   for dessert.

9. I have no **use** for   that broken radio.
10. I have no **juice** for   breakfast.

11. **You lie!**   I don't believe you!
12. **July**   is before August.

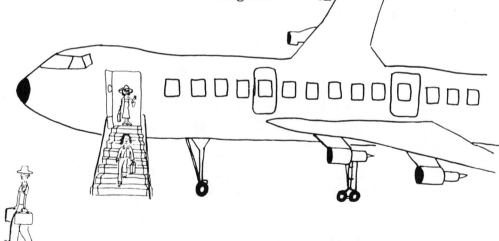

13. Can you see her **yet**?   Yes, there she is!
14. Can you see her **jet**   plane?

15. They stretch and **yawn**   when they wake up.
16. They stretch, and **John**   does his exercises.

Puppies Or Poppies? ESL Bingo ©1998 Elizabeth Kuizenga Romijn, Command Performance (510) 524-1191

ch/j Bingo Notes

Some language groups prone to problems discriminating between these two sounds:
Arabic, Cantonese, Cebuano, Czech, Dutch, Estonian, Fijian, Finnish, German, Hawaiian, Hebrew, Hmong, Indonesian, Italian, Korean, Laotian, Mandarin, Marshallese, Norwegian, Portuguese, Russian, Samoan, Spanish, Swahili, Swedish, Tagalog, Tamil, Thai, Tongan, Vietnamese.

Suggestions for clarification of the meanings of the sentences in this game:

1. A *batch* of cookies is a *group* or *bunch* of cookies all made together, at the same time, with the same ingredients. Suggested prop:* a *batch* of cookies! These could be for prizes today, or for everyone.

2. Refer to the picture of the policewoman.

3. In other words, what were they looking for? *Search* means *look for* something. *Search the building* means look *everywhere in the building.*

4. *Surge* means to come forward like a wave in the ocean. So the people moved all together, maybe because they were angry or excited.

5. Refer to the picture of the cat on a fence. A *rich* man is a man with a lot of money.

6. Refer to the picture of the cat on the *ridge* of a roof.

7. Refer to the picture of the dog on a *chain.*

8. *Jane's glasses* means *the glasses of Jane.* Jane is a woman's name. The -'s is possessive.

9. There is probably a *lunch bag* on a table in your classroom. Note that this is the possessive form of boy, not the plural.

10. Now we're talking about more than one boy. Demonstrate** *lung*ing at someone (suddenly moving toward them).

11, 12. *Cheer* and *jeer* are opposite sounds or shouts people make, depending on whether they are pleased or not. (Demonstrate *cheering* and *jeering*.)

13. Refer to the picture of the person choking on a fish bone.

14. "Please don't laugh at me."

15. Refer to the picture of the bearded chin.

16. Refer to the picture of the gin being mixed with juice.

ch/j Bingo

1. The policewoman has a **batch** of cookies.
2. The policewoman has a **badge** on her uniform.

3. Why did the crowd of people **search** the building?
4. Why did the crowd of people **surge** forward?

5. The cat is walking on the **rich** man's fence.
6. The cat is walking on the **ridge** of the roof.

7. He has **chains** around his neck.
8. He has **Jane's** glasses.

9. Did you see the boy's **lunch** on the table?
10. Did you see the boys **lunge** at the man?

11. The soccer fans **cheer** when they like the game.
12. The soccer fans **jeer** when they don't like the game.

13. I hope you won't **choke** on a fish bone.
14. I hope you won't **joke** about me.

15. I don't like his **chin**   with a beard.
16. I don't like his **gin** mixed with juice.

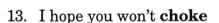

Puppies Or Poppies? ESL Bingo ©1998 Elizabeth Kuizenga Romijn, Command Performance (510) 524-1191

ch/sh Bingo Notes

Some language groups prone to problems discriminating between these two sounds:
Arabic, Cantonese, Cebuano, Danish, Dutch, Estonian, Fijian, Finnish, German,
Greek, Hausa, Hawaiian, Japanese, Javanese, Korean, Laotian, Mandarin,
Marshallese, Persian, Portuguese, Samoan, Spanish, Swahili, Swedish, Tagalog,
Tamil, Thai, Tongan, Vietnamese.

Suggestions for clarification of the meanings of the sentences in this game:

1, 2. If your students don't understand these two sentences, this game is too advanced for them. It would be better to do something else.

3. Refer to the picture of the woman trying to *catch* a fly ball.

4. *Cash the check* means *change the check for cash.*

5. If your students don't understand this sentence, this game is too advanced for them. Do something else (and offer them some corn chips to try.)

6. *Corn ships* are *cargo ships (boats) full of corn.* Refer to the picture of the *ship.*

7, 8. Refer to parts of your own leg and face, or pictures of someone else.

9. *Chop down* means *cut down.* See page 47—"Building a Fire"—of *Live Action English (Romijn & Seely, Berkeley: Command Performance Language Institute, 1997)* for a complete TPR wood-chopping sequence.

10. *Shop* means *go shopping, look for a coat to buy.*

11. Same as 1, 2 above.

12. *My share* means *my part (of something divided up).*

13, 14. *Saw* is the past form of *see.* Demonstrate *chew*ing.

15. Refer to the picture of the man with mismatched socks.

16. *Demonstrate* mashing potatoes.

ch/sh Bingo

1. I'm going to **watch**   TV.
2. I'm going to **wash**   my shirt.

3. She wants to **catch**   the ball.
4. She wants to **cash**   the check.

5. The corn **chips**   are delicious.
6. The corn **ships**   came to San Francisco.

7. My **chin** is part of my   face.
8. My **shin** is part of my   leg.

9. Are you going to **chop**   down a tree?
10. Are you going to **shop**   for a new coat?

11. I want my **chair**   to sit on.
12. I want my **share**   of the candy.

13. I saw her **chew**   her gum.
14. I saw her **shoe**   on the floor.

15. Will you please **match**   your socks?
16. Will you please **mash**   the potatoes?

ch/t Bingo Notes

Some language groups prone to problems discriminating between these two sounds: Brazilian Portuguese, Cantonese, Fijian, Hawaiian, Indonesian, Japanese, Samoan, Tongan.

Suggestions for clarification of the meanings of the sentences in this game:

1. Refer to the picture of the chickens chasing the rooster.

2. Why is this chicken so delicious?**

3. Suggested prop:* a *chip* of glass. A *chip* is a very small piece that has broken off of something.

4. Refer to the picture of the man looking at his nose.

5. *Chop* means *cut up.*

6. *Top* is a verb here. It means *put the sauce on top of the vegetables.*

7. Demonstrate *chew*ing with your mouth open and then closed.

8. If there is an emergency and everyone has to leave the classroom quickly, how many people can go thru the door at one time? *Please, only two at a time.*

9. *Teach* is what the teacher is supposed to do.

10. A person who *cheats* in a game *violates the rules;* he or she *tricks or deceives* the other players.

11. Refer to the picture of the person *catch*ing a fly ball. *Caught* is the past form of *catch.*

12. Refer to the picture of the *cat.*

13. Refer to the picture of the lit *match.*

14. Refer to the picture of the door*mat.*

15. Refer to the picture of the person catching a fly ball. Note that one knee has a hole in it and the other knee is *patch*ed.

16. Demonstrate *patting* someone on the back.

*Note: The more advanced your students, the less need there is for props (but it's still a lot of fun to use them.)

Note: Sometimes it's more efficient and just as productive to ***translate*!

ch/t Bingo

1. I don't know why the chickens **chased**   the rooster.
2. I don't know why the chickens **taste**   so good.

3. He's looking at the **chip**   of glass.
4. He's looking at the **tip**   of his nose.

5. Please **chop** the vegetables with this   knife.
6. Please **top** the vegetables with this   sauce.

7. Please **chew**   with your mouth closed.
8. Please, **two**   people at a time.

9. She didn't **teach**   me English.
10. She didn't **cheat**   in the card game.

11. Wow! What a good **catch**!   You caught the ball!
12. Wow! What a good **cat**!   He's very quiet!

13. We used the **match**   to start a fire.
14. We used the **mat**   to wipe our feet.

15. I'm going to **patch**   the hole.
16. I'm going to **pat**   you on the back.

Puppies Or Poppies? ESL Bingo ©1998 Elizabeth Kuizenga Romijn, Command Performance (510) 524-1191

th/t Bingo Notes

Some language groups prone to problems discriminating between these two sounds:
Bulgarian, Cantonese, Cebuano, Croatian, Czech, Danish, Dutch, Estonian, French, Georgian, German, Haitian Creole, Hawaiian, Hebrew, Hindi, Hmong, Hungarian, Indonesian, Italian, Japanese, Javanese, Korean, Libyan Arabic, Mandarin, Marshallese, Micronesian, Navajo, Norwegian, Pashto, Persian, Polish, Portuguese, Russian, Samoan, Serbian, Shanghainese, Swahili, Swedish, Tagalog, Tamil, Telugu, Thai, Tongan, Turkish, Urdu, Uzbek, Vietnamese.

Suggestions for clarification of the meanings of the sentences in this game:

1-2. Refer to the pictures. Please excuse the lack of color. Your students probably know what color *red* is, but if you'd like to color the *thigh* for item 1 and the *tie* for item 2 before you distribute the copies to the students, they'd probably get a kick out of it.

3. A *thick* coat is a *heavy, warm* coat. On a dog this means he has a lot of hair or fur.

4. Refer to the picture of the *tick*, an insect which sometimes spreads Lyme Disease by attaching itself to the skin of a person or a dog in order to drink their blood.

5-6. Refer to the pictures.

7. *Thought* is the past form of *think*.**

8. *Taught* is the past form of *teach*.

9. Refer to the picture. *We don't have any left* means *we have no more*.

10. Refer to the picture. *Tread* is the deeply grooved pattern on a tire that gives it traction. When there is no more *tread*, the tire is smooth. Suggested prop:* a piece of tire or the bottom of a shoe with good tread.

11-12. Refer to the pictures of the phone *booths* and the *boots*.

13. *Wealth* is *abundance*, for example *a lot of money*.

14. Refer to the picture of the man with a large bump on his head.

15-16. Refer to the pictures.

---

*Note: The more advanced your students, the less need there is for props (but it's still a lot of fun to use them.)

Note: Sometimes it's more efficient and just as productive to ***translate*!

th/t Bingo

1. His **thigh** is red   from the sun.

2. His **tie** is red.   His shirt is white.

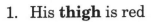

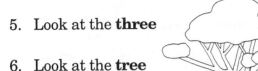

3. The dog has a **thick**   coat.
4. The dog has a **tick**   in his neck.

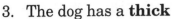

5. Look at the **three**   babies.

6. Look at the **tree**   in the park.

7. They always **thought**   you were married.
8. They always **taught**   English.

9. We don't have any **thread** left   for our sewing machine.
10. We don't have any **tread** left   on our tires.

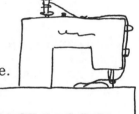

11. Show me which **booth**   you want to sit in.

12. Show me which **boot**   is for the left foot.

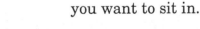

13. He got his **wealth**   by working hard.

14. He got his **welt**   from a car accident.

15. She has a big, warm **hearth**   in front of the fire.

16. She has a big, warm **heart**   full of love.

Puppies Or Poppies? ESL Bingo   ©1998 Elizabeth Kuizenga Romijn, Command Performance (510) 524-1191

th/s Bingo Notes

Some language groups prone to problems discriminating between these two sounds: American Spanish, Arabic, Bulgarian, Cantonese, Cebuano, Danish, Dutch, Estonian, Finnish, French, Georgian, German, Haitian Creole, Hausa, Hawaiian, Hebrew, Hindi, Hungarian, Indonesian, Italian, Japanese, Javanese, Korean, Mandarin, Micronesian, Navajo, Persian, Polish, Russian, Samoan, Shanghainese, Swedish, Tagalog, Tamil, Tongan, Urdu, Vietnamese.

Suggestions for clarification of the meanings of the sentences in this game:

1. Refer to the picture of the *thimble*—protection from the needle when sewing by hand.

2. Refer to the heart.

3. My brother is always hungry.

4. *Sinks* means *goes down in the water.*

5. If your students don't understand this sentence, this game may be too advanced for them, or...**

6. *Sank* is the past form of *sink*. Refer to the picture of the sinking boat.

7. Show the students your left *thumb*. Then cover it so you *can't see it.*

8. Refer to the copy of a grocery receipt with the total obscured. *Sum* means *total.*

9. *Faith* is a *belief* and *trust* that something is true.**

10. If your students don't understand this sentence, this game is too advanced for them. It would be better to do something else.

11. When someone talks too much we say they have a *big mouth.*

12. Refer to the picture of the *mouse* under the chair.

13. Refer to a calendar, pointing to the 10th day of the current month.

14. *The tense part of the movie* is the part that makes you nervous.

15-16. Refer to the pictures. Please excuse the lack of color. Your students probably know what color *green* is, but if you'd like to color the *moth* for item 15 and the *moss* (on the rocks) for item 16 before you distribute the copies to the students, they'd probably get a kick out of it.

**Note: Sometimes it's more efficient and just as productive to translate!

th/s Bingo

1. Here is a **thimble** — to protect your finger.
2. Here is a **symbol** — of my love.
3. My brother always **thinks** — it's time to eat.
4. My brother always **sinks** — when he tries to swim.

5. I know they **thank** — you for your help.
6. I know they **sank** — the boat.
7. I can't see the **thumb** — on my left hand.
8. I can't see the **sum** — of the prices.
9. I remember her wonderful **faith** — in God.
10. I remember her wonderful **face** — and hair.
11. You have a big **mouth**! — You talk too much!
12. You have a big **mouse** — under your chair!
13. This is the **tenth** — day of the month.
14. This is the **tense** — part of the movie.
15. The beautiful green **moth** — is flying above my head.
16. The beautiful green **moss** — covers the rocks.

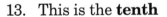

Puppies Or Poppies? ESL Bingo ©1998 Elizabeth Kuizenga Romijn, Command Performance (510) 524-1191

sh/s Bingo Notes

> **Some language groups prone to problems discriminating between these two sounds:** Cantonese, Cebuano, Estonian, Fijian, Finnish, Greek, Hawaiian, Hmong, Indonesian, Italian, Japanese, Javanese, Korean, Marshallese, Samoan, Tagalog, Tamil, Tongan, Vietnamese.

Suggestions for clarification of the meanings of the sentences in this game:

1. Refer to the picture of the walnuts. *They're shelling* means *they're taking the shells off.*

2. If your students don't understand this sentence, this game is too advanced for them. It would be better to do something else.

3. *Show me how* means *teach me.*

4. Refer to the picture of the dress on the sewing machine.

5. She wrote a letter. Where is it? (*Wrote* is the past form of *write.*)

6. Referring to the English alphabet, ask the students where the *letter C* is; that's right, it's the third letter.

7, 8. Refer to the pictures of the target and the woman in a business suit.

9. A *sheet* of paper is a *piece* of paper.

10. *Take a seat* means *sit down.*

11, 12. Refer to the pictures of the old *shack* and the *sack* (*bag*) of potatoes.

13, 14. Refer to the pictures of the man shopping for shoes and the dripping wet boy.

15. A *ship* is a large *boat.*

16. Demonstrate (pantomime) taking a sip of wine.**

**Note: Sometimes it's more efficient and just as productive to translate!

sh/s Bingo

1. They're **shelling**   the walnuts.
2. They're **selling**   their car.

3. Can you **show**   me how to swim?
4. Can you **sew**   a dress?

5. Where is the letter **she**   wrote?
6. Where is the letter **C**   in the alphabet?

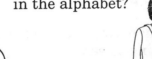

7. I never saw her **shoot**   at the target.
8. I never saw her **suit**   for work.

9. Please take a **sheet**   of paper.
10. Please take a **seat**   in the office.

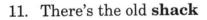

11. There's the old **shack**   where they live.
12. There's the old **sack**   of potatoes.

13. He's **shopping**   for shoes.
14. He's **sopping**   wet!

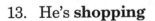
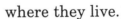

15. I'm going to take a **ship**   to Hawaii.
16. I'm going to take a **sip**   of wine.

Puppies Or Poppies? ESL Bingo ©1998 Elizabeth Kuizenga Romijn, Command Performance (510) 524-1191

f/th Bingo Notes

Some language groups prone to problems discriminating between these two sounds: Arabic, Burmese, Cantonese, Cebuano, Danish, Estonian, Finnish, Georgian, Hebrew, Hindi, Italian, Javanese, Korean, Micronesian, Navajo, Persian, Polish, Russian, Samoan, Spanish, Swedish, Tagalog, Tamil, Telugu, Tongan, Turkish, Urdu, Uzbek, Vietnamese.

Suggestions for clarification of the meanings of the sentences in this game:

1, 2. Refer to the picture of the fish.

3. I don't need paper or books; I only need my lunch.

4. *Thirst* is what you feel when you need something to drink. *Hunger* is what you feel when you need something to eat.

5, 6. *Fought* is the past form of *fight*. *Thought* is the past form of *think*. Refer to the pictures.

7. *Enough* means *sufficient*. Sometimes when people talk too much we say, "That's enough." *Fred* is a man's name.

8. Refer to the picture of the three spools of *thread*.

9. *Free* parking is parking you don't have to pay for.

10. *Breakfast* is the first meal of the day, usually in the morning. *Lunch* is the middle meal, in the middle of the day. *Dinner* is the evening meal.

11. An *offer* is a *proposal*.

12. An *author* is a person who writes books. *Children's books* are books written especially for children.

13. *Wrote* is the past form of *write*. A *deaf child* is a child who can't hear.

14. *A death in the family* means someone in the family died.

15, 16. Refer to the pictures. Ruth is a woman's name.

f/th Bingo

1. This fish has a long **fin**  and tail.
2. This fish has a long **thin** 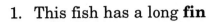 body.

3. This lunch is all I need for my **first** day at school.
4. This lunch is all I need for my **thirst** and my hunger.

5. The boys **fought** over the pretty girl.

6. The boys **thought** over the job opportunity.

7. That's enough, **Fred**. Don't say any more!
8. That's enough **thread** 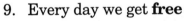 to make a dress.

9. Every day we get **free** parking.
10. Every day we get **three** meals: breakfast, lunch, dinner.

11. That's a wonderful **offer**! Thank you!
12. That's a wonderful **author** of children's books.

13. He wrote a sad story about a **deaf** child.
14. He wrote a sad story about a **death** in his family.

15. Here's a picture of the chimney, **roof** and windows of my house.
16. Here's a picture of the chimney, **Ruth**. Do you see smoke?

f/p Bingo Notes

Some language groups prone to problems discriminating between these two sounds: Arabic, Burmese, Cebuano, Georgian, Hausa, Hawaiian, Hindi, Indonesian, Javanese, Kannada, Korean, Marshallese, Navajo, Pashto, Samoan, Tagalog, Tamil, Telugu, Tongan, Turkish, Uzbek, Vietnamese.

Suggestions for clarification of the meanings of the sentences in this game:

1. Suggested prop:* a bottle of perfume or cologne.

2. Refer to picture of the *pine* trees.

3. *Fare* is the *money* or *price* to ride the bus.

4. If your students don't understand this sentence, this game is too advanced for them. It would be better to do something else.

5. Suggested prop:* a toy car with 4 doors that open.

6. Refer to the picture of the beat-up old Volkswagen.

7. *Flyers* are airplane pilots.

8. Refer to the picture of the *pliers*.

9. Suggested prop:* any kind of *fan* (electric, or make one of paper).

10. Suggested prop:* any kind of cooking *pan*.

11. Refer to the picture of the *fin* of the shark.

12. Refer to the picture of the jacket with the lapel *pin*.

13. Same as 4 above.

14. Suggested prop*: an orange—demonstrate peeling it. See page 44 of *Live Action English (Romijn & Seely, Berkeley: Command Performance Language Institute, 1997)* for a complete TPR orange-peeling sequence.

15, 16. Refer to the picture of the *pork* and beans dinner and place setting.

*Note: The more advanced your students, the less need there is for props (but it's still a lot of fun to use them.)

f/p Bingo

1. Can you smell the **fine**   perfume?

2. Can you smell the **pine**   trees?

3. I don't have the **fare**   for the bus.

4. I don't have the **pair**   of pants.

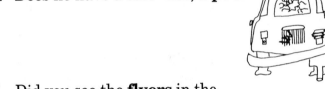

5. Does he have a car? Yes, a **four-**   door.

6. Does he have a car? Yes, a **poor**   old VW.

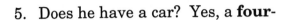

7. Did you see the **flyers** in the   airplane show?

8. Did you see the **pliers** in the   tool box?

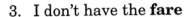

9. She needs a **fan**   because it's so hot.

10. She needs a **pan**   to cook the food.

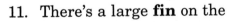

11. There's a large **fin** on the   back of the shark.

12. There's a large **pin** on the   front of her jacket.

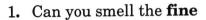

13. How do you **feel**   today?

14. How do you **peel**   an orange?

15. Where did you get that **fork**   and spoon?

16. Where did you get that **pork**   and beans?

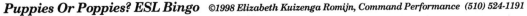

Puppies Or Poppies? ESL Bingo   ©1998 Elizabeth Kuizenga Romijn, Command Performance (510) 524-1191

f/v Bingo Notes

> **Some language groups prone to problems discriminating between these two sounds:** Arabic, Burmese, Cantonese, Cebuano, Estonian, Finnish, Georgian, Hawaiian, Indonesian, Japanese, Javanese, Korean, Marshallese, Micronesian, Navajo, Pashto, Tagalog, Tamil, Thai, Vietnamese.

Suggestions for clarification of the meanings of the sentences in this game:

1. A *ferry* is a boat especially for crossing a river or lake where there is no bridge. Often you can drive your car onto the ferry, too.

2. Another way to cross a lake is in an airplane.

3. *Fan* is short for *fanatic*, someone who loves a sport or music group or famous person.

4. Refer to the picture of the *vans* (small busses) full of baseball players.

5. The *final exam* is the *last examination (or test)*.

6. *Vinyl* is a kind of material sometimes used to cover floors. Maybe you have some on your classroom floor, or the students may have it on their kitchen floors.

7. My *offer* is something I proposed or invited or offered to her. She *refused* means she said *no*.

8. Movie *reviews* are *critical evaluations* of movies.

9. Refer to the picture of the *rifle*.

10. Refer to the picture of the boxing match. *Rival* is *opponent*.

11. Refer to the picture of the earthquake *fault*.

12. Refer to the picture of the bank *vault*.

13. *Safe* means *secure*, the opposite of *dangerous*.

14. *Save* means *retain*, *keep*, or *rescue*.

15. Refer to the picture of the tree *infested* with insects.

16. When you buy something hoping it will have a higher price or value in the future, you are *investing*.

f/v Bingo

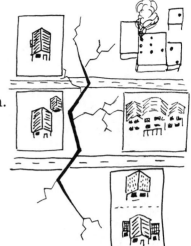

1. You can cross the lake in a **ferry**   boat.
2. You can cross the lake in a **very**   slow airplane.

3. The baseball team has a lot of **fans**   who love to watch.
4. The baseball team has a lot of **vans**   for traveling.

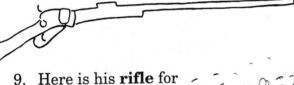

5. This is the **final**   exam for this class.
6. This is the **vinyl**   to cover the floor.

7. Did you hear her **refuse**   my offer?
8. Did you hear her **reviews**   of the movies?

9. Here is his **rifle** for   shooting practice.
10. Here is his **rival** for   the boxing match.

11. Where is the **fault**   from the earthquake?
12. Where is the **vault**   in the bank?

13. The word **safe** is   an adjective.
14. The word **save** is   a verb.

15. Thousands of them **infested**   the apple tree.
16. Thousands of them **invested**   their money in gold.

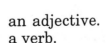

Puppies Or Poppies? ESL Bingo ©1998 Elizabeth Kuizenga Romijn, Command Performance (510) 524-1191

w/v Bingo Notes

Some language groups prone to problems discriminating between these two sounds:
Arabic, Bulgarian, Burmese, Cantonese, Croatian, Czech, Danish, Dutch, Finnish, German, Greek, Gujarati, Hausa, Hebrew, Hindi, Hungarian, Indonesian, Japanese, Javanese, Laotian, Mandarin, Norwegian, Pashto, Persian, Russian, Samoan, Serbian, Swedish, Tamil, Thai, Turkish, Urdu.

Suggestions for clarification of the meanings of the sentences in this game:

1. Refer to the picture of the *wicker* chair.

2. A *vicar* is a *priest* in the Protestant Church of England (Episcopalian) or sometimes in the Catholic church.

3. Why did they go to school? To learn English; that's why.

4. *Vent* means *release* or *express*. If you don't *vent* your anger in some way, it will make you very tight and even sick.

5. Refer to the picture of the *whale* in the swimming *pool*.

6. Refer to the picture of the wedding couple, the woman in a *veil*.

7. Worse means *more bad*. Maybe your story is bad, but his story is *more* bad, but we *never* say *more bad*; we say *worse*.

8. Suggested prop:* copies of a song with several verses.

9. Point out the four directions: north, south, east, *west*. Point out who or what is on the west side of your classroom.

10. Refer to the picture of the man in the *vest* and tie.

11. *A while* is *some time*.

12. Refer to the picture of the *vial* from a laboratory. Blood is the red liquid inside your body.**

13. If your students don't understand this sentence, this game is too advanced for them. It would be better to do something else.

14. Refer to the picture of the *vine*, a plant that climbs on something else.

15. Refer to the picture of the rowing crew in their boat.

16. A *rover* is someone who travels all the time or moves often to a new place.

*Note: The more advanced your students, the less need there is for props (but it's still a lot of fun to use them.)

**Note: Sometimes it's more efficient and just as productive to translate!

w/v Bingo

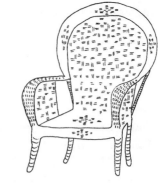

1. You can see the **wicker**   chair.

2. You can see the **vicar**   in the church.

3. That's why they **went**   to school.

4. That's why they **vent**   their anger.

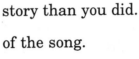

5. She has a **whale**   in her pool.

6. She has a **veil**   over her face.

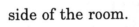

7. He wrote a **worse**   story than you did.

8. He wrote a **verse**   of the song.

9. That's my father in the **west**   side of the room.

10. That's my father in the **vest**   and tie.

11. We took a **while**   to get here.

12. We took a **vial** 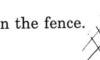   of blood.

13. The **wine** is   delicious.

14. The **vine** is   growing on the fence.

15. She's a **rower**   on the team.

16. She's a **rover**;   she never stops traveling.

Puppies Or Poppies? ESL Bingo ©1998 Elizabeth Kuizenga Romijn, Command Performance (510) 524-1191

b/v Bingo Notes

Some language groups prone to problems discriminating between these two sounds: Arabic, Burmese, Cantonese, Cebuano, Farsi, Greek, Hmong, Indonesian, Japanese, Javanese, Korean, Marshallese, Navajo, Spanish, Tagalog.

Suggestions for clarification of the meanings of the sentences in this game:

1, 2. *TB* is short for *tuberculosis*; *TV* is short for *television*.

3. Refer to the picture of the boat in the water.

4. *He has my vote* means *I'm going to vote for him.*

5. Refer to the picture of the *ballet* performance.

6. Describe *valet parking* to those not familiar with it: where someone parks your car for you in front of an expensive hotel or restaurant, especially in a crowded downtown location. The person who parks the car and brings it back to you is called a *valet*.

7, 8. *Demonstrate hiding* something. *Hid* is the past form of *hide*. Describe a cover (sheet, blanket, bedspread) on a bed and a cupboard (permanent cabinet) in a kitchen.

9. Refer to the picture of the taxi *cabs*.

10. Refer to the picture of the *calves*.

11. *Bowels:* intestines (point to your gut.)

12. *Vowels:* a, e, i, o, u.

13. Refer to the picture of the *berries*. A *berry farm* is a place where berries are grown (produced).

14. If your students don't understand this sentence, this game is too advanced for them. It would be better to do something else.

15. Refer to the picture of the *baseball* and *bat*.

16. Describe a situation where someone is thanking another person for several things (such as friendship, a place to live, a car), including a job opportunity.** Note that the letter *f* is pronounced *v* in the word *of.*

Note: Sometimes it's more efficient and just as productive to translate!

b/v Bingo

1. Do you have **TB**? Yes,   I'm very sick.
2. Do you have **TV**? Yes,   we watch it every night.

3. He has my **boat**   in the water.
4. He has my **vote**   for his election.

5. I'm happy to see **ballet**   performances.
6. I'm happy to see **valet**   parking.

7. They hid the money in the **cupboard**   in the kitchen.
8. They hid the money in the **cover**   on the bed.

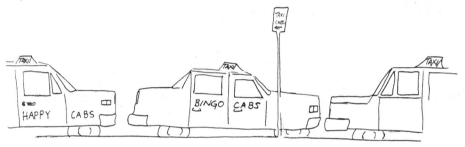

9. The **cabs** are waiting for the   passengers.
10. The **calves** are waiting for the   cow.

11. What's wrong with your **bowels**? I have   indigestion.
12. What's wrong with your **vowels**? I have   trouble with pronunciation.

13. They have a **berry**   farm.
14. They have a **very**   happy family.

15. You gave me **first a ball**   and then a bat.
16. You gave me, **first of all**,   a great job.

Puppies Or Poppies? ESL Bingo ©1998 Elizabeth Kuizenga Romijn, Command Performance (510) 524-1191

b/p, d/t, g/k Bingo Notes

Some language groups prone to problems with these three distinctions in final position: Arabic, Cantonese, Dutch, Estonian, Fijian, Finnish, German, Haitian Creole, Hawaiian, Hmong, Indonesian, Italian, Korean, Laotian, Mandarin, Marshallese, Micronesian, Navajo, Persian, Portuguese, Samoan, Shanghainese, Spanish, Tamil, Thai, Tongan, Turkish, Vietnamese.

Suggestions for clarification of the meanings of the sentences in this game:

1, 2. Suggested props:* a *full bag* and a *tired back* are easy to find in most classrooms.

3. Refer to the picture of the *pig* eating.

4. Refer to the picture of the woman *picking up* the baby.

5. *Demonstrate hiding* in a closet or something.** *Hid* is the past form of *hide.*

6. Refer to the picture.

7, 8. *Rode, wrote:* past forms of *ride, write.*

9. *Hard: difficult*

10. Refer to the picture of the *heart.*

11-16. Refer to the illustrations. Suggested prop** for #13: A piece of cloth full of holes. Suggested prop** for #14: a piece of rope full of knots.

*Note: The more advanced your students, the less need there is for props (but it's still a lot of fun to use them.)
Note: Sometimes it's more efficient and just as productive to ***translate*!

b/p, d/t, g/k Bingo

1. My **bag** is   full.
2. My **back** is   tired.

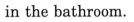

3. Watch her **pig**   eat.
4. Watch her **pick**   up the baby.

5. My brother **hid**   in the bathroom.
6. My brother **hit**   the ball.

7. They **rode** the   bus.
8. They **wrote** the   letter.

9. This is a **hard**   Bingo game.
10. This is a **heart**   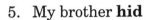   full of love.

11. Is there a **cub**   with the mother bear?
12. Is there a **cup**   on the table?

13. His **robe** is full of      holes.
14. His **rope** is full of   knots.

15. Put the **cab**   in the garage.
16. Put the **cap**   on your head.

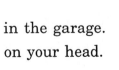

Puppies Or Poppies? ESL Bingo ©1998 Elizabeth Kuizenga Romijn, Command Performance (510) 524-1191

d/th Bingo Notes

Note: Some of this vocabulary borders on being too obscure for beginning and intermediate students. Please use discretion in using this game with students whose English may not be advanced or sophisticated enough to handle it. (Suggestions gladly accepted for simpler, stronger items for this game.)

Some language groups prone to problems discriminating between these two sounds:
Bulgarian, Cebuano, Cantonese, Croatian, Czech, Danish, Dutch, Estonian, Farsi, Fijian, Georgian, German, Hawaiian, Hebrew, Hindi, Hmong, Hungarian, Indonesian, Italian, Japanese, Javanese, Libyan Arabic, Korean, Laotian, Mandarin, Navajo, Norwegian, Pashto, Persian, Polish, Russian, Samoan, Serbian, Shanghainese, Spanish, Swahili, Swedish, Tagalog, Thai, Tongan, Turkish, Urdu, Vietnamese.

Suggestions for clarification of the meanings of the sentences in this game:

1, 2. Refer to the pictures.

3, 4. If your students don't understand these two sentences, this game is too advanced for them. It would be better to do something else.

5. *Wordy* means *there are too many words*. It could be said more concisely, more elegantly, without so many words.

6. *Worthy* means *good enough*. *Worthy of publication* means *good enough to print in a book to sell*.

7, 8. Refer to the pictures.

9. Ask the same question about a student who is absent from your class today.

10. *They've* is a contraction for *they have*. (If your students have not yet been presented with the present perfect tense, you may have to translate this sentence.)

11. *Load the truck* means *fill the truck*. Refer to the picture of the truck being loaded.

12. *Loathe* means *hate*, the opposite of *love*.

13. *Doze* means *sleep a little*. Demonstrate dozing in class.

14. Review *this, that, these, those*, if necessary.

15. Refer to the picture of the horses being fed. *Fodder* means *cheap food for animals on a farm or ranch*.

16. If your students don't understand this sentence, this game is too advanced for them. It would be better to do something else.

d/th Bingo

1. Look at the **ladder** to the roof.
2. Look at the **lather** on his face.

3. On Christmas **day** we eat a big dinner.
4. On Christmas **they** are going to Mexico.

5. This poem is **wordy**. It has too many words.
6. This poem is **worthy** of publication.

7. I want to eat the cookie **dough** before we bake it.
8. I want to eat the cookie, **though** my stomach is full.

9. Do you know why **Dave** isn't here?
10. Do you know why **they've** gone home?

11. I know he's going to **load** the truck.
12. I know he's going to **loathe** that movie.

13. She's going to **doze** during the class.
14. She's going to **those** stores over there.

15. Here's **fodder** for the horses.
16. Here's **Father**! He's home!

z/th Bingo Notes

Note: Some of this vocabulary borders on being too obscure for beginning and intermediate students. Please use discretion in using this game with students whose English may not be advanced or sophisticated enough to handle it. (Suggestions gladly accepted for simpler, stronger items for this game.)

Some language groups prone to problems discriminating between these two sounds:
Arabic, Bulgarian, Castillian Spanish, Cantonese, Cebuano, Czech, Danish, Dutch, Estonian, Fijian, French, Georgian, German, Greek, Hausa, Hawaiian, Hebrew, Hindi, Hungarian, Indonesian, Italian, Japanese, Javanese, Korean, Laotian, Mandarin, Micronesian, Navajo, Polish, Russian, Samoan, Shanghainese, Swedish, Tagalog, Tamil, Thai, Tongan, Urdu, Vietnamese.

Suggestions for clarification of the meanings of the sentences in this game:

1. *Tease* is similar to *play*, but when you *tease* a cat, for example, you never let the cat get the toy you are playing with. Refer to the picture of the baby and the cat.

2. When a baby's teeth are growing in, it causes pain and sometimes fever. We call it *teething*.

3, 4. If your students don't understand these sentences, this game is too advanced for them. It would be better to do something else.

5. *Breeze past* means *pass easily*. Demonstrate *running*.

6. Demonstrate *breathing hard* or being out of breath, as if you have just been running.

7. *Zen* is a form of Buddhism and meditation.

8. *First I went to Japan, and after that I went to China.*

9. Refer to the picture of the sailboats.

10. *Bathe* is a verb. It means *take a bath*.

11. *Seizing: taking.* Someone stole a car and now the police are taking it.

12. *Seething: violently angry, ready to explode, like a volcano.*

13. Point out all the places the letter *Z* appears in today's written lessons.

14. Refer to the groupings of chairs in your classroom.

15. Refer to the picture of the courtroom scene. The person who *sues* is the person who tries to win an argument or disagreement by bringing it to court.

16. Refer to the picture of the man playing guitar and singing. *Soothe* means *bring comfort, calm, relief* for someone who is nervous or tense or in pain.

z/th Bingo

1. The baby is **teasing**   the cat.
2. The baby is **teething**.   Her mouth hurts.

3. At the department store, **closing**   time is 9 p.m.
4. At the department store, **clothing**   is expensive.

5. If you run, you will **breeze**   past that slow man.
6. If you run, you will **breathe**   hard.

7. I visited a place in Japan. **Zen**   is the religion there.
8. I visited a place in Japan. **Then**   I went to China.

9. People who live in California **bays**   love to sail.
10. People who live in California **bathe**   every day.

11. The police are **seizing**   the stolen car.
12. The police are **seething**.   They're angry!

13. The teacher put a lot of **Z's**   in the lesson.
14. The teacher put a lot of **these**   chairs together.

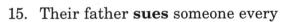

15. Their father **sues** someone every   year in court.
16. Their father **soothes** someone every   time he sings.

z/s Bingo Notes

Some language groups prone to problems with this sound discrimination: Arabic, Cantonese, Cebuano, Danish, Dutch, Estonian, Fijian, Finnish, German, Greek, Haitian Creole, Hawaiian, Indonesian, Italian, Javanese, Korean, Laotian, Mandarin, Marshallese, Micronesian, Norwegian, Samoan, Spanish, Swedish, Tagalog, Tamil, Thai, Tongan, Vietnamese.

Suggestions for clarification of the meanings of the sentences in this game:

1, 2. Write the alphabet across the chalkboard and then point out the ordinal positions of the letters *c* and *z*.

3. Point to your *knees*; *weak* is the opposite of *strong*.

4. Your *niece* is the daughter of your sister or brother.**

5, 6. Refer to the pictures of the cat and the iced soda.

7. Mimic the sound of *buzzing* insects.

8. *Leaving* means *going away from*.

9. If you've never played Bingo before with this class, you may need to explain what a *prize* is.

10. In other words, how much does it cost?

11. *Peace on Earth* means *no more war*.**

12. Refer to the picture of the *peas*.

13. Refer to the picture of the man lying on the sofa.

14. Refer to the picture of the bride in a *lacy* dress. Suggested prop:* A photograph of a lacy dress, or better yet, a piece of lace, to be sure the students understand what lace is.

15, 16. *Demonstrate raising* your hand and *racing* (running fast) down the street.**

*Note: The more advanced your students, the less need there is for props (but it's still a lot of fun to use them.)
**Note: Sometimes it's more efficient and just as productive to *translate*!

z/s Bingo

1. In the English alphabet, **Z** is the   last letter.
2. In the English alphabet, **C** is the   3rd letter.

3. What's wrong with your **knees**?   They're weak.
4. What's wrong with your **niece**?   She's sick.

5. Look at the **eyes**   of that cat.
6. Look at the **ice**   in my soda.

7. Can you hear the **buzz**   of the insects?
8. Can you hear the **bus**   leaving the station?

9. What's the **prize**   for this Bingo game?
10. What's the **price**   of this jacket?

11. I hope there will be **peace**   on Earth.
12. I hope there will be **peas**   for dinner.

13. Wow, what a **lazy**   man!
14. Wow, what a **lacy**   dress!

15. They're going to **raise**   their hands.
16. They're going to **race**   down the street.

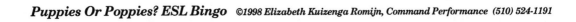

Puppies Or Poppies? ESL Bingo ©1998 Elizabeth Kuizenga Romijn, Command Performance (510) 524-1191

BINGO!

BINGO!

BINGO!

Puppies Or Poppies? ESL Bingo   ©1998 Elizabeth Kuizenga Romijn, Command Performance (510) 524-1191

BINGO!

		FREE		

About the Vimala Font

The representations of handwriting appearing in this book are set in the Vimala Alphabet Font which is a template for the Vimala Alphabet.

Vimala Rodgers is an educator, author, handwriting expert, master alphabetician, and a peak performance coach. In 1991 she founded The Vimala Rodgers Institute of Integral Handwriting Studies as the international center for training in the science of graphotherapy. Drawing from a lifetime of research and study, Rodgers is pioneering the development of a technology that focuses on personal transformation thru healthy handwriting. She has developed programs which combine her vast knowledge of handwriting and of the personality with her expertise in the psychology of peak performance.

Acknowledged for centuries as a diagram of the unconscious mind, handwriting is a clear reflection of the lens thru which we see life: self-image. As a master alphabetician and handwriting expert, Vimala Rodgers is intimately familiar with the meaning of each stroke of the pen.

For that reason she has designed The Vimala Alphabet. It is the only writing system that uses handwriting not only as a method of written communication, but also as a means of developing those traits necessary to build a successful and fulfilling life.

"Since pointed V's represent discernment, T's crossed on the top reinforce healthy self-esteem and the willingness to excel, and uncluttered circle letters support honesty, I have designed an alphabet that reflects the most positive aspects of ALL the letters, for in writing them, the writer, on a subconscious level, reaffirms the aspects they represent."

—Vimala Rodgers

index